THROUGH
THE UNKNOWABLE

THROUGH THE UNKNOWABLE

Family Life with Depression,
Alcohol, and Love

a memoir by
ELSA CAMPION, M.D.

VANTAGEPress
NEW YORK

This is a work of non-fiction. However, the names of the people and places have beed changed to protect those involved.

Cover illustration by Ann Brandenburg Zeman
Cover design by Molly M. Black
Vantage Press and the Vantage Press colophon
are registered trademarks of Vantage Press, Inc.

Published by Vantage Press, Inc.

419 Park Ave. South, New York, NY 10016

Manufactured in the United States of America
ISBN: 978-0-533164-97-4

Library of Congress Catalog Card No: 2011910420

0 9 8 7 6 5 4 3 2 1

to my children

to family and friends,
teachers and patients,
who nourished me along the journey

Penetrating so many secrets,
we cease to believe in the unknowable.
But there it sits nevertheless,
calmly licking its chops.

—*Minority Report, H.L. Mencken's
Notebooks,* Knopf, 1956

Contents

ALARM

Floodlights carved shadows on the ice-skating rink in the darkness of early evening, the sound of Christmas songs from loudspeakers matching the bright colors of coats and scarves. I watched my daughter Luce totter on her skates. Having turned thirteen in November, she was almost my size, with gangly limbs and the large hands and feet that come from my Flemish grandfather. But her narrow chest and smooth cheeks under straight-cut hair were those of a child. Rounding a corner, she skated toward me, and her ghostly pale face shone, drawn and distant. I clutched the rink's wooden fence, trying to read in my daughter's face what troubled her.

My husband and I went to the mountains for a week in December 1987, with our two youngest children. As if we were a regular privileged family on holiday. When she'd heard that her older sister would spend this vacation not with us but with friends, Luce asked to stay with her friend Amy. We had to be stubborn to make her come, stating the obvious: that Anna was a senior in high school and not an eighth grader. Besides, Luce seemed unwell, nervous and skittish, and I wouldn't have left her two hours away in the valley where we lived.

She'd met Amy early that year, a small-boned, spirited redhead with a quick smile. At first the two girls often came to our house after school, setting up plays in the garage or jumping on the trampoline. During the fall, though, Luce went to Amy's for more and more extended visits.

She spent the whole weekend after Thanksgiving there. She returned home on Sunday as the afternoon light was fading and I stopped setting the table to embrace her. We kissed on each cheek, as family members did in my home in France. That's when I noticed her mottled skin and the shadows under her eyes. "Luce, what's wrong?"

"I'm okay, Mom," she answered breezily. She dropped a stuffed shoulder bag on the floor and took off her coat. Her sweater hung from her shoulders as from a clothes hanger.

"You're losing weight."

"Nah. You worry too much." She lugged her bag toward her bedroom.

I turned to her father, James, who was dicing vegetables at the sink. "She doesn't look good."

He shrugged. "She's doing fine."

But I had been worried for a while. As a psychiatrist, I knew all too well what kids could get into in our laid-back town in the Pacific Northwest, with its hippie flavor and easy flow of street drugs. I picked up the phone and dialed Amy's mother. "What did the girls do?" I asked after thanking her for inviting Luce. "She looks a little sick. Did they go out?"

No, she answered. The girls had done art projects and watched movies. "Maybe they stayed up too late."

James stopped me when I told him I was still uneasy. "You've got to trust people," he said with a suspicious sidelong glance. I thought maybe we had stopped talking about Luce. Memories of his drinking years, before he quit for good, were indeed in my thoughts.

He stirred the vegetables in a wok with quick strokes, dashed in sesame oil that sizzled and smoked, then raised sharp blue eyes to my face. "She gets good grades, she comes home from school on time. Cut her some slack." Sibilant sounds whistled through his clenched jaws. James was at home when the children came back from school in the afternoons and chatted with them about their days. I was at my office or the hospital until late. His look told me that his opinion should prevail.

I agreed that I was overprotective of Luce and reminded myself to trust her. She had proved her strength in dealing with repeated eye surgeries for the congenital cataracts that had blinded her when she was four. After the opaque lenses were removed from her eyes, she could see colors in bright hues but, without glasses, shapes had no more detail than what one sees from the bottom of a swimming pool. At twelve, she convinced her ophthalmologist that she was responsible enough to handle contact lenses. She threw away the heavy thick-lens glasses that magnified her bright blue eyes and caused classmates to make fun of her. From then on she chose not to let new acquaintances know how little she could see, determined to do everything they did, like bicycle or ski. Years of training and smarts allowed her to compensate for poor vision, though not always, of course. She once rode her bike into the bumper of a parked car, which she had thought was moving. She conspired with her friends and siblings to hide such small mishaps from her father and me.

At the mountain in December, Luce and her brother David skied under bright skies with their dad. She admitted to David that on a slope, when she became airborne, she squeezed her eyes shut "because I can't see anything anyway."

I didn't ski and spent time walking and reading. Thoughts of Luce troubled me. While we were washing our hands before a meal, I examined her reflection, thin and pale in the bathroom mirror.

"Tell me why you look so sick," I said. "Are you doing drugs?"

She pulled away, eyes averted and lips tight. "I—am—all—right," her words spoken low but with biting emphasis. "I'm not doing anything wrong." Then she walked off to the dining room.

She ordered a thick rare steak. She teased David, who had recently decided to be a vegetarian, by dangling a bloody piece of meat in front of his nose. Leaning toward him, her eyes crunched and lips pursed like a crone, she spoke in a raspy stage whisper. "Do you want this, little boy? Good protein for you."

David twisted his face in disgust, but laughter shone in his brown eyes and a light blush colored his cheeks before he moved his head away from the offending sight and smell. He clearly loved the attention and worshipped Luce, three years his senior, with her wicked streak of nonconformism.

When she heard us laugh, she swiveled her head toward James and me with a triumphant glance. She knew how to appease her parents: be nice to your little brother, be funny, and eat all your dinner. Her confidence in our loving bias toward her softened her smile, and tenderness spread through me like honey.

I decided to give her time, to be gentle, and to enjoy myself as best I could. Joy was in the details, I thought one afternoon when Luce and I rode horses, details like the roundness of the slow rental horse under my thighs, the fermented smell of its warm body in the cold air of the forest, the strength of Luce's upright stance as she rode, her grin when she turned to look at me, caressing the dark mane of her horse then leaning forward to embrace its neck.

On Christmas Day, the day before leaving the mountain, we opened presents and Luce looked stronger, more animated. The week of rest, exercise and pleasant exchanges with her brother and us had brought a bloom to her face.

But I was still on edge. The kids slept in the sitting room of our suite. When I came in that evening to tell them to turn off the TV and go to sleep, I found the room empty and my heart seized. I remember the moment as a freeze-frame taken from a horror movie, black and white, without sound: children have disappeared, and their mother's mouth gapes open as she cries out for them. The sound of my own children's muffled laughter, an instant later, brought color and motion back to the scene. I walked to the source of the noise, a big Murphy bed that they had folded back up against the wall, hiding inside. When I pulled it open, out tumbled pillows, a sheet, and two children ecstatic at the success of their joke. The sight and sound of their happiness healed the sharp stab of fear.

JUST A CHILD

How do I recapture the foggy messiness of my emotions the winter after Luce turned thirteen? I was a mother, watchful. I noticed pale skin, clouded eyes. I read the message of defeated sloping shoulders, of shuffled feet when my daughter went to the fridge to get milk for her morning cereal. I was also a psychiatrist, trained to ask myself "What does this mean?" and to come up with hypotheses: "What if she is depressed? Could it be drugs?"

I had listened to countless addicts and depressives in my practice. But personal experience spoke even louder. Addiction and depression were intimate enemies in our families. Luce might share more with her father than the gene for blue eyes, or have inherited from me the propensity for severe depression.

My recollections of Luce's early adolescence are often shady. Which mother wants to burden her child by noticing and remembering every little thing that goes wrong? I knew that fear was a devious informant, clouding perceptions and twisting judgment. Often, when I said that I worried about them, James and the children complained that I didn't trust them. Certainly I was wrong at times, but at others I had been right to worry.

So, what was I to do? Returning home after our vacation, I checked Luce for fever and signs of infection, asked about pains and other symptoms: none. I would keep watching and, if she continued to look ill after the holidays, would take her to our family doctor for a thorough examination.

A few days after Christmas, Anna was with friends, David playing outside with the neighbor boys, and when Luce, lonely, begged to go to a slumber party, James and I agreed.

Early the next morning, when I thought Luce was still sleeping at her friend's house, the doorbell rang. James and I converged from different rooms into the front hall. Through the glass door, I saw against the lead-gray sky the silhouette of a young man, one arm around Luce, the other raised toward the bell. I searched his face for recognition, but he was a stranger, around twenty, dressed in warm clothes. His eyes remained cast down and he said nothing, only gently eased Luce forward, when James opened the door. She seemed skinnier than the day before, a thinly stuffed rag doll unable to hold her head up, too diffident to look me in the eye as she stumbled in. The young man had already turned around and was running back to his car.

A few thick, incoherent words and the acid smell of booze on Luce's breath made it clear that she was drunk, wasted. She didn't argue when I put her in my car and drove to the lab for blood and urine analysis. I don't remember asking James' opinion. Enough lies. I wanted some facts.

The results came by phone a few hours later, about midday on New Year's Eve. I went to the kitchen where James was making coffee. A bowl with a bit of Froot Loops-colored milk remained on the counter from David's late breakfast, and music wafted from his room. Luce was still asleep.

"Ready for lunch?" James asked.

I shook my head. It was hard to speak. I didn't want to hear my own words. "Shouldn't be a big surprise after this morning, I guess. The tests are positive for a lot of alcohol and cannabis." I heard James' sharp intake of breath, and continued. "Otherwise, no sign of a medical disorder."

So here were the facts I had wanted, but what to do with them now? James and I stared at each other. I felt shaky inside. I have no recollection of what either of us said next, but soon we were walking together toward Luce's room.

I raised the blinds and sat on her bed to wake her. Sella, the old Siamese cat who slept beside her, rose and walked across her chest to leave the room. Luce sat up, rubbed her eyes and face. James paced her bedroom, littered as usual with the clothes she dropped when she undressed, scattered shoes and music tapes, and he finally sat in a beanbag chair.

Luce grimaced at the light coming through the window, leaned back on the pillow, and shut her eyes. I shook her shoulder. "Wake up, we need to talk." She moaned a little when I told her about the lab results. "Tell us what happened."

She wouldn't speak at first, only mumbling in response to questions. Once she started talking, however, she seemed almost eager to tell her story, sitting up with her eyes open. She didn't look directly at either of us, though, but only stared at the winter sky through the window.

The first time she had used drugs, she said, was the previous summer, with friends from school in the old graveyard at the bottom of the hill where we lived. The place suited the kids' fascination with ghost stories and horror movies, which I had tried in vain to discourage. Her small junior high group hung out with older "druggies" who offered some of what they had. We already knew from Anna that such practice was standard—the youngest didn't have to pay. I still get hot with indignation when I think of that practice of handing out free samples to create a market of faithful customers for the drug cartels.

James sank deeper into the beanbag chair, making a squishy sound. His face was haggard, his eyes wide. "Why would you do that?" he asked.

"I wanted to know what's the big deal with drugs. Just curious," she said in a bizarrely flippant tone. James and I exchanged a glance of recognition. She had always been curious—and fearless.

Little by little, she gave us details. She'd tried LSD, mushrooms, pot, and alcohol. It was easy to hide her use from us during the summer, when we thought she was out playing with neighborhood friends like a regular twelve-year-old. "I could just wait to come home until I was okay," she said. After classes started and the weather turned rainy, she often smoked pot at Amy's house. "Her mom has plenty, she doesn't mind. Sometimes we did it before going to class."

"That can't be!" James, who'd been a teacher, exclaimed. "Teachers would have noticed, they would have told us."

"One of them lets kids crash in a cubicle behind his classroom." She laughed. "He's an old hippie, he doesn't care." Later David, who went to the same middle school, told us that this teacher even joked about Luce's spaciness. What chance did parents have?

The school counselor had paired Luce, who signed up for a peer counseling program, with Amy, who had just moved from California. The counselor told us later that she guessed Luce would be a good influence on Amy, who was "at risk" due to her own history of drug use and her living alone with an addicted mother. We might have approved, but were not given a chance to supervise the girls because the counselor never told us about the arrangement. When I confronted the counselor later, she defended her duty to protect Amy's anonymity. But she had not protected our daughter, not been there to check on her during the long summer of experimentation with drugs. Good intentions gone bad. Bad judgment unquestioned.

On the afternoon of New Year's Eve, in Luce's bedroom, meagerly lit by the dense gray light of winter, my head swam in a confusion of images and questions. I could not accept what I heard, the drugs, the lies. It couldn't be real. Even if it was, I didn't want to let the reality permeate my mind. There was surely a way to return to the world of childhood, which had existed less than thirty minutes before.

I remembered how Anna had called Luce "an honest little thief." When she was three or four, Luce would sneak into her sister's room to take toys or candy. But as soon as Anna, returning from school, confronted her with a dramatic scowl, Luce told her what she had done and gave back the toys. Now, sitting rigid on her bed, forehead bent forward as a young horse pulling a heavy load, our honest little liar went on telling all the bad stuff of the last few months.

Instead of watching videos or playing board games at Amy's, as we'd been led to believe, the girls had gone to parties—plenty of them—where they met friends from school plus many others. I asked in a tight voice what I didn't really want to know. Yes, Luce said, there was sex, mostly older guys with young girls. I made a note to test her for sexually transmitted diseases, trying not to picture this child, our broken baby, with shady men like the one who'd driven her home that morning. I got up from her bed where I'd been sitting, disgust and anger tasting sour in the back of my throat, to look out the window at the oyster-colored sky of this last day of the year. "There's lots of booze," Luce added after a silence, her voice dreamy. "I like it, I like being drunk."

I was afraid, helpless, and didn't know what to say. She was just thirteen, for heaven's sake. James and I locked eyes and both moved without a word to hold Luce as she shivered and cried. She seemed as fragile as a sparrow fallen off its nest. She hiccupped "I am sorry" between deep, teary sighs and finally fell asleep. Her face on the pillow was hollow, ageless, drained of life, yet smooth and somehow at peace, as if relieved to have told the truth. It was hard to leave the room, but we had to discuss what to do for our child.

How could I, how could we, have missed so much? It was my job to notice those things, after all, and James had worked for four years as a special education teacher in a state hospital. He attended recovery groups for alcoholics; both his parents, their seven children, and every uncle were in the same boat, some in recovery, others not. The curse of the Irish.

We personally knew many young people whose dependences had flared like a gasoline-fueled wildfire in their early teens. Now Luce was caught in the inferno. It seemed to have grabbed hold of her as soon as she was exposed. In less than six months of use, she had been overcome.

And so were we. We moved around the kitchen like balls on

a pool table, bumping against the counter to get a cup of coffee, passing each other on the way to the fridge for milk, sitting for a minute at the table, then up again to get a piece of bread. "Did you eat lunch?" "Don't remember." Finally giving in to exhaustion, we settled on chairs to talk.

James sighed, staring into the coffee cup he held with both hands. "What a shitty illness," he said. I nodded, thinking of the heavy toll alcoholism extracted from his family. His voice trailed off, low and sad: "As if she hasn't had enough." I knew he thought of the numerous eye surgeries for cataracts, the thick glasses.

I needed to move before grief overtook me. "She hasn't done it long, maybe she can recover." I shook myself and stood up on unsteady legs, glancing at the gathering darkness outside.

"Yeah," James said quietly, barely moving his lips, "Maybe."

And he nodded when I added, "I'll call SHARP."

That was the adolescent recovery program of the local hospital. On the phone with the admission nurse, I could hear my voice shift from Mom's, quivering with repressed sobs, to Doctor's, methodically outlining history and asking for precisions about the program. I sat straighter after the call: we had a plan. Treatment was to start on January 2nd. I'd be on vacation till then, not having to care for patients at the office. The time off was a good thing, as I felt more than insecure: deskilled, unable to trust my judgment.

James started fixing dinner while I went to explain to David what was happening. He had stayed in his room all afternoon, door firmly shut. I'd been vaguely aware of the music he played while we talked to Luce in her bedroom down the hall, but my mind was not on him. The air in his room was thick, I thought when I entered, as if nothing had moved there for hours, the window darkened by big old fir trees, trails of fog hanging on their heavy branches. David was sitting on his bed in near darkness, hugging a pet. Was it the rabbit or his white rat that year? or Mao the tomcat? I don't remember. But I remember the fear in his eyes and how he shrank from my touch when I went to hug him, as if he didn't want to catch what devastated me.

For the rest of the day we checked regularly on Luce. Her hands shook, she shuffled like an old lady from bed to bathroom, and she had to be urged to drink water and eat a little soup. She nodded meekly when told about the treatment center. We all went to bed early.

Before dawn the next morning, New Year's Day, I found Luce nearly unconscious in her bed, taking short rough breaths. Her eyes rolled back when I lifted the lids to look at them. I raised her head and shoulders to hold her very close, putting my lips close to her ear. "What did you do? What did you take?"

She turned her head, eyes still closed, toward the bathroom, and raised a limp hand in that direction. "Aspirin." If she'd taken enough, she could die from acidosis.

I wrapped her in a blanket and held her shivering, clammy body against mine as James drove us to the hospital.

David stayed home alone, a nine-year-old boy who couldn't possibly grasp what shook his world. Years later he told me, "I remember the day that I decided I would stop feeling. It was when Luce tried to kill herself the first time and you all went crazy. I built a wall of concrete around me."

Hate does not come easily to me, but I hated one woman then. At the hospital, in January 1988, when Luce was hooked up to IV fluids to restore physiologic balance, Amy and her mother showed up in her room.

I grabbed the mother's arm and walked her out to a corridor by the elevators. It was empty and dark, lit only by a window on each end and a weak ceiling light.

"You lied to me," I said, close to her face. I remembered telling her I was worried about Luce, asking why Amy didn't come to our house anymore. "I called many times to ask you what they did at your place."

The woman backed up to the wall, close to the elevator, looking up and down the empty hallway. Her pasty round face was pale under the neon light and her eyes looked afraid, but she grinned a ridiculous smile, in a servile expression of appeasement. I pushed on. "You lied. What did you think you were doing?"

Her features wavered but she kept her stupid grin, upper front false teeth too white next to the others, as if she had been punched in the mouth years before. I kept my eyes on her face and finally she answered, "They were going to try anyway. I was afraid they'd be on the street and some man would hurt them. I gave them some of my stuff and kept them home." Her voice almost begged. "They were safe."

The crazed logic of the addict. There was nothing to discuss. I turned and left her. Back in the room, I sent Amy away.

Soon, Luce was out of immediate danger from the aspirin. Our family doctor came by to examine her and I recounted what Luce had told us the day before, about the drugs and sex at parties. Afterward, the doctor reassured us that our daughter was in good physical health and had not been sexually active—one less worry. Still, the central problem remained.

Luce entered drug and alcohol treatment the next day. Walking with her into the adolescent recovery unit brought me immediate relief: she would be safe for the time being. But sitting in the nurse's office to fill out admission questionnaires felt odd, disorienting. On the one hand, the scene I saw through the windowed partition into the central room of the unit was familiar. Patients shuffled in from the corridor that led to their bedrooms to join activities. Half-completed puzzles lay ignored on card tables. A few people stared out of the windows at sodden, dark bushes in the small garden while most patients gathered around tables with tall urns of coffee and juice bottles. Some were engaged in conversations with counselors who wore similar open and concerned expressions, as if those expressions were a uniform. I had been there many times, not only in this particular building where I did consultations, but in countless other buildings with the same architecture, the same smell of boiled coffee and stale cigarettes, and the same impression of aimless activity.

But what was my little girl doing here, amid older adolescents with shaved heads, tattoos, and attitude? How did we get here?

Before

Each January in my new country, after I moved from France in 1969, I had to register at the US Post Office as a resident alien. Our mailman joked about my not looking like the extraterrestrial from the movie. Many aspects of my new life surprised me, but none felt as foreign as the immersion in the drinking subculture of my husband's family and close friends.

During the months that we had lived together in Paris after having met the previous year at a conference, James and I kept no liquor at home, as was my habit. The few times he drank too much at a party, I thought that it was because Americans were unaccustomed to wine. Thirty-one that year, I was neither young nor innocent, but had no personal knowledge of alcoholism, having only treated the physical consequences of abuse in hospitals. I didn't yet know James' long history of dark moods and drink. A few hours before our wedding, in our bed in the middle of the night, I heard his voice, very low. "I need to tell you now," he said in an urgent whisper, then paused. I tensed, not moving until he spoke again. "I think I may have a problem with alcohol." I remember folding my knees tight close to my chest, frozen in the dark silence that lasted a long time. What am I supposed to do with this? I thought. I don't have time to think about it. What do I tell my family? It's too late.

So I pushed the information away. I convinced myself that

everything would be better once we settled in his home in Kansas. I focused on the future we had planned, on my new adventure at a great school, and even more on the promise of having children.

We were ecstatic when I soon became pregnant. So many new things to discover: new husband, new language, new culture, first pregnancy, first year of residency. So much promise. But Sunday visits with James' family confounded me. I presumed that we'd eat around one, the usual time for a Sunday meal at my home, but time dragged on until late afternoon, during which the seven siblings and their mother consumed drink after drink. A super-size bottle of Scotch stood on the kitchen counter close to the refrigerator, and one family member or the other would go pour another shot or two and add ice. I never liked liquor, and I think this is when I began to feel nausea at the very sound of ice cubes clinking against glass.

I had never been around so much systematic drinking, and observed what happened with dismay. All but the youngest were drunk by mid afternoon, and they held conversations about politics, philosophy, or literature that progressively unraveled, yet no one seemed to notice. Their refined mother cut everyone down to size with her sharp tongue and the elegant dismissal of raised eyebrows. James' sweet little sisters lost their liveliness, and the brothers argued, in polite tones at first, but only at first. Sarcasm corroded the conversation like acid rain and I didn't want to participate for fear of inflaming the debate. I could not understand much of what was said, but my confusion had little to do with English. I could only notice that the simplest words had unexpected meanings and weight.

Upon returning home after one more such Sunday, I stood as tall as I could in front of James to tell him that I hated the stupid drunkenness, and asked why he had changed. "You didn't do that when we were in Paris."

"What's wrong with you?" he answered. "We're just having fun. It's the weekend, for heaven's sakes," and left the room.

Neither of us could understand the other's point of view. James drank more and more as my pregnancy progressed. Late at night,

sitting up against the pillows in our bed, his face lit in the darkness with every pull of his cigarette, he spoke of his father in a
voice filled with sadness, and of his own qualms about becoming a
father, even though he looked forward to the baby. "I don't want
my kid to grow up in a home like mine," he said. His dad had
worked long hours at his restaurant while the children grew up,
and he remained distant even at home. After losing his business
to bankruptcy, when James was in his late teens, he disappeared
for months on end. James, the oldest son, would occasionally be
called by a sheriff to pick up his father after he'd ended up in jail
for drunkenness.

I stubbornly tried to focus on the good parts: the keenness of
my husband's mind, the arresting beauty of his eyes, brilliant as
the noon sky of a clear winter day in Kansas. His straight, slender nose, the blackberry scent of his skin, the clean planes of his
naked back, the softness of his lips. But it was too late now: I was
stuck with the memories of rants and accusations. "You don't listen to me. You don't support me; you don't care." The voice that
stayed with me had metallic and sibilant tones, the eyes the blaz-
ing intensity of righteousness, like those of the abolitionist John
Brown on the frescoes of the state capitol.

At first that persona disappeared after a good night's sleep.
The next morning James did not remember his outbursts and was
charming. I did my best, as a fledgling psychiatrist overly impressed
by the power of catharsis, not to judge or challenge. I went along
with his need to discount the influence of liquor and agreed that
being hurt by his parents caused his rage. I think that, at some
level, I admired his vivid display of anger. At least he complained
when he felt mistreated, whereas a few years back I had let myself
sink deep into the cold muck of profound depression.

In fact, I joined James in denying, for as long as I could, that
drinking was the main part of the problem, hoping to keep our
life steady.

From the moment Anna was born, in the spring of 1970, I could
look at no one else. If being in love with a husband who puzzled me

was confusing, maternal love shone clear from the start. Obvious and absolute, it launched me into another dimension of being.

James had acted as my Lamaze coach, attentive and businesslike until the birth. His whole face softened when he saw his daughter. Tears mingled with an amazed smile as he delicately placed a hand on her. He had been around babies all his life and handled Anna with competence and assurance when we came home a few days later, whereas I had to learn every trick, like testing the bath water with an elbow or setting a cloth on my shoulder before burping the baby. He tempered his drinking markedly, enough to give me hope.

We made the best of our life. We bought the VW camper that would be a faithful companion on many road trips across the continent. We were both in therapy by then. My analyst led me on explorations of another kind, through the immensity of thought, memory, pain, dreams, and hope. I rediscovered the sense of life's vast promise, like a pioneer's courageous purpose to walk into the unknown, and was determined to be happy. I still hated the importance of alcohol in James' life, the look and smell of it, the sound of ice cubes in the glass, the money it cost. But he drank much less than before Anna's birth and I became expert at keeping distance from his weird mix of leadenness and inflammable temper when he'd had too much.

At the end of my residency I decided to take some time off to recover from the forced-march pace of the training. James continued to teach special education at the state hospital and we chose to stay put, among friends and family. Early in 1974, I became pregnant again and was filled with delight. James seemed as happy as I was, yet, as the pregnancy progressed, so did his drinking.

I couldn't believe it. First, I pointed out to him that he was drunk more often, as if somehow he hadn't noticed his own behavior. Then I told him he should stop and suggested ways of getting help. Not surprisingly, he appreciated none of my interventions. Finally, one morning as he entered the kitchen bleary from the previous night's excess and I waddled around fixing Anna's breakfast, I harangued him. "You promised you'd control yourself. And look at you. I feel cheated."

He slowly turned, rage in his eyes. "I wouldn't need to drink if you were not such a shrew." Ashamed of my own acerbity, I wondered if he was correct.

By summer vacation he was drinking all day. One evening in our bed, before passing out, he told me in a heartbreaking voice, "I love you and Anna so much, but I can't do anything different." For the first time I believed that he indeed had no control. I had no idea what to do then, except hold him. Much later he would tell me about that time. "I knew that drinking would destroy my life—but later, some other day. And not drinking today would kill me. I would immediately self-destruct, I was convinced of that." I've since heard similar statements from others, the utter conviction that the poison, the destroyer, is necessary to survive.

A bout of acute pancreatitis, frequently associated with alcoholism, brought James to the hospital. While I visited him one day, a couple came in, bearing expressions that curiously mixed timidity with assertiveness. The man, compact with a round, florid face, went to James, who sat up in his bed, face barely less white than the sheets, drawn from the sharp pain in his belly.

"I want to tell you about something that changed my life," the man said. "I think it might change yours too." He handed James a pamphlet with the Twelve Steps and a list of meeting places and times. His wife came up to me quietly and gave me a small piece of paper. I looked into her benign, ordinary face, aureoled by a bad perm, at her gentle eyes. "Call me if you want to go to a meeting. It's hard to love an alcoholic. We know." I felt that she did indeed know and tucked her phone number in my pocket.

One afternoon, two weeks later, I picked Anna up from preschool and we walked home. She chatted busily about all she'd done with her friends and teachers. The September light was golden and the air carried a welcomed coolness after the summer.

Back home, I called out to James to ask when he wanted to eat. Receiving no response, I went upstairs and saw him sprawled helter-skelter on our bed, dead drunk. Angrier by the second, I went to sit on the bed and found myself holding him by the shoulders, his head lolling to one side, eyes opening for a second, forehead creased by the effort, then heavy lids closing again. I was shaking him and screaming in his face that he must stop that nonsense when I felt a small hand tug at the hem of my skirt.

Anna stood straight and said in a factual tone of voice, "Mama, I don't think he can hear you."

I stared at her without understanding for a second. I hadn't heard her come up the stairs, I had forgotten all about her, I didn't know the world still existed, only my anger. I read the wisdom in the astute, dark eyes of my four-year-old daughter, so vulnerable in her strength, and shame inundated me. In a flash I pictured myself, moments earlier, as a raging dog sinking its teeth into flesh, shaking its prey.

Terrified by the image, I stood up, grabbed Anna's hand, and fled the house. I had never thought I would act as my mother used to, out of control with anger from crazed helplessness. Had I learned nothing from watching her? Anna and I walked to a friendly neighbor who agreed to keep her for the rest of the day. Back home, I didn't go upstairs or listen for sounds coming from the bedroom, but phoned the gentle woman from the hospital. She took me to a meeting that evening.

There I heard that alcoholism is a "cunning, baffling, powerful" condition, one I hadn't caused and couldn't control. Next, in a quiet, plain voice, one of the women told me that, just as I was not responsible for my husband's drinking, he was not responsible for my unhappiness. I pulled back my head as if slapped, yet, just as fast, the clarity and common sense of this statement gave me hope. Of course! I could decide for myself the course my life would take, even if James didn't get better. I knew this in my heart, but somehow that knowledge hadn't made its way to my brain. My mother had taught me that you never leave someone whom you profess to love, even if you're both miserable. Being miserable is the least you can do to demonstrate your own goodness and strength of character. I would later see this as a perversion of self-esteem.

In September 1974 and two months before the baby was due, my priorities were clear: to take care of Anna and of my health until the birth, then take care of the newborn. I had divorce papers drawn up by a lawyer, but decided to wait to assess whether to leave James until I had found my stride with the two children. In the meantime, support groups helped to keep my thinking clear, and biofeedback training to temper my fretfulness. I stopped checking on James, turning my head away from the accumulation of empty bottles in the basement when I went to do the laundry. I also turned my heart away from him, leaving us both sad and lonely.

We were alone in the middle of the night when Luce was born. James stayed at my side during labor and delivery but looked ill, thin, and shaky. We hardly spoke. I singlemindedly focused on my body's sensations and the task of helping the baby along. Looking back, I remember surrendering totally to the physical perception of the life force working within me toward its ultimate manifestation: a new being. I experienced a kind of bliss.

Luce was a strong baby with a placid expression and a round head barely covered in fine, golden fuzz. She appeared thoroughly content to eat, sleep, and look with a delighted smile at the world through eyes that became as intensely blue as her father's. She liked being held and I could hardly get enough of her trusting abandon, almond-lotion smell, and silky skin.

One month after her birth, having come terribly close to killing himself, James drove to the hospital and signed himself into the alcoholism treatment program his doctor had long recommended. It was part of the teaching hospital where I had trained, and I was self-conscious the first time I went for a joint meeting with his treatment team. Talk about blowing your anonymity! But we soon reaped the benefits of blasting open our not-so-secret secret shame. Friends and colleagues gathered around us with love and encouragement. James and I became regulars at recovery meetings. Hope and trust returned, and love, a trickle at first, flowed again.

I recall the next few years as singularly happy, amid much support. The soundtrack of those years replays in my mind: laughter and children's shouts from the yard, Melina Mercouri singing "Never on Sunday" in Greek while James and I sat together on the couch by the window in the late afternoon sun, tired of the day, watching Luce in her Jolly Jumper. Before walking, Luce loved to bounce in that contraption and looked like a miniature circus aerialist, squealing with pleasure.

Luce became the pet of a group of young adults, alcoholics and addicts, who gathered in our home every week. She was held, played with, talked to and fed cookies. But, when she learned to talk, she took to quoting here and there some of what she'd heard during the discussions. Because it is essential that what participants share in a meeting remain confidential, it became clear that she shouldn't attend anymore.

When James told her, she looked up at him with her enamel-blue eyes fixed square on his face. "Why?" How could she understand the concept of anonymity?

His explanations didn't cut it; she was indignant at being barred from the fun. Firmly planted on her strong little legs, head slightly lowered like a young goat ready to butt, she stood her ground. "I won't bother anybody. I'll be quiet."

When she finally understood that she couldn't argue her way back in, she announced, before leaving the room with all the wounded dignity that a three-year-old could muster, "When I grow up, I'm going to be an alcoholic, and then I can go to meetings!"

We all laughed. Then.

FEAR AND HOPE

I n early summer 1988, three months after finishing drug and
alcohol treatment, Luce, then thirteen and a half, went to a
Vision Quest camp for young people in the Oregon high desert,
east of the Cascade Mountains.

On the day she returned, bright-eyed, she tossed wrinkled
clothes and camping gear around the kitchen in wide-arced gestures while rattling on, in a strong voice colored with joy, about
the smell of sagebrush under the burning sun and sleeping in
open air, listening to the howls of coyotes and to rustling sounds
of unidentified origin, but that might be of rattlesnakes. She had
done all the walks and rock climbs, undeterred by her poor sight.

That night at dinner I forgot to eat, staring into her animated face as she recounted her adventures. I feasted on her dark
eyebrows, one of which flew up like a tiny bird wing just as my
father's had, on the blush under her smooth, tanned cheeks, her
plump lips that opened fully over wide teeth. She laughed loudly
and I felt that my quirky, affectionate little girl was back.

Before bed, she and I sat in our backyard hot tub in the intimate dark of night. I floated happily in pleasure from the heat, the
sound of bubbling water and the occasional touch of our hands or
knees. To the east, we watched a huge orange moon rise in majesty
over the mountains. In a deep and quiet voice Luce told me how
she loved the full moon, the light of which never hurt her eyes, as

the sun's did, and bathed the world in beauty. Then she began to cry and added softly, "It was weird one day. They sent us to walk alone and told us to be open to meet our demons. I got kind of lost and thirsty. I didn't take any water. It was really hot." I had to strain to hear her voice, low and hypnotic. I didn't want to speak, even when she stopped.

"I saw them, Mom," in a whisper, then silence. Too long a silence. I tried to see her expression in the faint moonlight but she bent down her head, dark hair hiding her face. A fleeting image came to me of the pointy teeth of a grotesque Hieronymus Bosch demon, biting lost souls.

"What did you see, my love?"

She shook her head slowly side to side several times, saying nothing, and when I took her in my arms she shuddered. The shudder shook me to my foundations. I remembered holding a patient's hand while she writhed from the assault of memories of horrendous childhood abuse. A silent voice screamed inside me that no thirteen-year-old should have to suffer such visitations. Luce never did tell me what she had seen, and I have often scanned my own memories of her childhood for possible suspects.

I would not know for many years how often inner demons visited her and how she chose not to reveal them. At times I wonder if her silence was really a choice or an automatic strategy, as if refusing to illuminate her worst fears made her safer, like not feeding a dangerous beast that prowls around at night. I have often enough turned away from what I wished didn't exist, so who am I to blame her?

Luce had walked out of the hospital with her head high the previous February, strong and determined. Every week until she got her license, James or I drove her back to the adolescent treatment center, where she led a group for newly admitted patients. She told them what she had used and how it had brought her to the point of wanting to die, like many of the kids who were listening to her. And then she shared what helped her to remain clean and sober.

Luce sponsored many young people in recovery, and over the years at meetings I've met several of them who credited her with saving their lives. She attended several meetings a week, called her sponsor regularly, and went to dances with sober buddies instead of to drunken parties. At home, she and her father frequently talked about "the program" and grew closer.

I too went to meetings, the same kind that I had grown familiar with to deal with James' drinking. What was it that I found in the program and wanted my daughter to receive? Not the literal wording of the steps, whose religiosity had raised my hackles at the start. I call myself a dedicated atheist, but am mostly anticlerical. I think leaders of any church gain power from promises they can't keep. I choose not to use the word God when I discuss my spiritual beliefs because I don't trust how organized religions all too often exploit that very word for their own gain, guaranteeing answers to the mysteries of life, death, and pain. I am convinced that no human mind can encompass those great mysteries, and made a deliberate choice not to raise my children in a church.

But I am a believer in the principles that I have seen at work in recovery meetings, and it no longer disturbs me to hear whatever language of faith others choose to express those principles. Gratitude, fellowship, humility, trust, honesty, and courage: these words evoke clear memories of individual voices telling their stories, of artless faces veiled in tears or intent with purpose, and of heads nodding in concert along with knowing laughter when someone reveals a stupid thought or a thoughtless act that others recognize in themselves.

I had met too many addicts, both friends and patients, to expect that the Twelve Steps would work for everyone, every time. And yet, I knew enough people who had emerged whole from years of despair, thanks to those principles, that I would not deny Luce the hope that she might receive similar gifts from her recovery and find peace of mind. As far as I could tell back then, she did.

The path was far from smooth, far from clear, but James and I relied on our stubborn faith in the power of healing and on the dogged courage to do all we could. What could I have known then about the hidden depth of Luce's pain? How could I have guessed it? It felt as dangerous to live in fear as it was to hope, so, at times, I pushed away my fears for her future, not wanting to lose heart. By making each day as good as I could, choosing activities that had made us happy before, I hung on to the appearance of normalcy, trusting it would carry her along to happiness.

One Sunday morning that August, I sat on our deck with a cup of coffee, watching the mountains to the east, feeling the day gather heat. David came out of his room, laughing with the friend he'd invited over and feeding bits of his breakfast cereal to the rat sitting on his shoulder.

"Do you want to see him dance?" he asked his friend, who nodded eagerly.

David put on a cassette tape of rock music and the rat started bopping his head and shoulders up and down in sync with the music. "No way," said the boy.

"Yes!" I loved David's exultant tone. He selected another tape and, sure enough, the rat's movements followed the different beat. James put down his newspaper to laugh with the boys.

I wanted our whole family to laugh together on that summer day. "Let's go to our swimming hole," I suggested, referring to the place we went to when the weather was warm enough. "I'll get the girls."

Anna shook her head. "I'll be with my friends." She would soon leave for college in New York and was making good-bye rounds. I didn't insist that she accompany us to the swimming hole; much of the time, she seemed already gone.

But Luce looked pleased, especially when I said we should ask Sophie, her best friend since grade school, to come along. Time to throw some picnic food in a basket, gather suits and towels, kiss Anna good-bye, and pick up Sophie. We were on our way.

From a flat boulder in the middle of a mountain stream, I watched the girls, skinny long legs and flat bodies, bump and grind on a pretend stage as they belted out a disco tune. Then, good little tomboys, they dove into the cold water, splashing David and his friend, and dared the boys with shouts and challenges to their ten-year-old budding manhood—"Are you a man or a mouse?"— to jump from the highest rock. The remembered cacophony of that day is sweeter to me than any music.

There was much I didn't see. I told myself that Luce had only used drugs and alcohol for a short time and that the longer she stayed sober while growing up, the better she'd feel. James and I focused on her dedication to recovery. The psychologist she met every week, a specialist in treating adolescents, was equally hopeful. We had no idea what she wrote about in her journal.

A blue spiral notebook with the Mead brand name on the wrinkled cover, dated April through November 1988, looked like any schoolwork implement when I found it at the bottom of her closet years later. But opened, it felt radioactive from the destructive power that emanated from the scrawled, dark words.

One minute I can love and cope and I see positive things in my life and in my family. The next minute I want to run, and if I can't I panic. I get totally edgy at the twitch of an eye. Sometimes despair. Sometimes thoughts of using or suicide. These things are dangerous to feel. I am so used to thinking through conflict. Analyzing myself. But now my emotions have control over me. I never had to control them before, I never felt them. But now I do, and I don't know shit on this subject. Time to learn.

It was eerie to recognize myself in her words: accustomed to thinking through conflict, to analyze, but also knowing the power of dangerous feelings. I had made a grave suicide attempt at twenty-six, and during later times of severe depression, I feared I might not be able to resist a strong suicidal impulse. I intended to share this part of my life with Luce at some time, to offer her the hope that she would recover as well as I did, but I hadn't done it yet. I held off until she was older, wanting to protect her innocence. "She's only thirteen," I must have thought, "I don't want to burden her," not knowing she was already bowed under the same burden.

What came next in her journal, though, was foreign to me. Were those the demons too scary to describe to her mother, or her therapist?

> I don't understand why I'm having these visions of slashing people. People I like. I can't decide but I am sure I will end it. It would be so easy if I had a gun. Probably poison. Today I live on the Ray Bradbury Planet, the one that rains for 7 years, then is sunny for 2 hours. I don't want to wait that long.

She liked horror stories and made outrageously gory comments, as do many adolescents to show they're tough, like the gallows humor my friends and I fell into early in medical school while dissecting our first cadaver. But what of the regular visits Luce and a friend made to a taxidermy shop on the outskirts of town? And her insistence to stop the car to drag roadkills to the grassy side of the road, giving them a sort of abbreviated funeral? Those were oddities we all chose to gently make fun of, to ignore really, attributing them to Luce's fondness toward animals. Just a quirky girl, I thought, fascinating and endearing. Did my love for her blind me when I should have watched her like a hawk, probed the reasons for those quirks, thereby possibly uncovering her preoccupation with death?

> Suicidal thoughts are telephoning my head. For no basis or reason. It just pops into my head. Some people get inspirations like "I think I'll go watch TV," I get "I think I'll go hang myself in the garage." Is this strange? Tell me, I don't know.

I recognized the thoughts from my own suicidal times and had heard similar expressions from many patients. Insanity creeping up, the early markings of a severe depression that later takes over. I knew that the slide into depression is an utterly lonely time, an experience most sufferers are unable to share with others. But that knowledge couldn't keep me from cringing when I read the next entries.

What am I going to do? People said I looked distracted today. Please give me a stronger wall. I've got to stop writing and plaster a "Hi Mom! Hi Dad!" smile so that they will be satisfied. They are satisfied = they leave me alone. They think everything's OK = I'm much better off. I never cried, I never lost control.

I chose—was it ever a fully conscious choice any more than Luce's own choice to hide?—I chose to be satisfied with her apparent happiness, to drink in the honeyed sweetness of her smile and the way she leaned into my embrace. If pressed by questions she didn't wish to answer, she would look at me gently and bat her hand as if shooing an importune fly, and I would stop. I was reluctant to displease her and so was James. If we gave in to her, for example by letting her go out on a school night after first refusing, the reward was to see her, as she strode fast toward her room before we changed our mind, look back over her shoulder and let out a light cascade of delighted laughter. Such gifts kept us coming for more.

How could I possibly think of Luce's journal as a gift? Yet this word came to my mind as I read it, followed by its opposite: "I hate it, I hate it," whose propulsive force sent me pacing the room, throat tight and hands trembling. I wanted to run away, squeeze my eyes shut, and press palms over my ears. Still, I wanted to know all I could about her, so the girl I lovingly remembered would be real, full, true to life.

So I continued to read.

What is going on? It's leading to what? Death—Insanity? I want to scream but I can't. Inside I'm shredding up and it's chaos. But I can't show how I feel—shitty and fucked up—I hate this.

I can't let it out because God knows what would happen. It wouldn't be safe. "I can handle everything—I don't need anyone." Are these not true anymore? NO, I won't accept it.

What do I now make of all this? I see a kind of crazy courage in a very young girl. I guess, without proof, that she did not disclose the intensity of her troubles partly because she was embarrassed that they did not make sense, that she first wanted to figure things out on her own. But maybe I only think this because it's what I did after my suicide attempt.

Mostly, I have the overwhelming desire to go back and shake my daughter: "Go ahead, fall apart, we'll put you back together. Please my love, show us the pain inside, we'll soothe it." Am I now the insane one? Could we, parents, doctors, have done that? I have witnessed the considerable healing powers of life and trusted them implicitly to be at work in my patients, yet all the while knowing I could neither ensure nor predict a positive outcome for any particular person. Her father and I, and her therapist, would have tried every which way to help Luce, but in any case none of us guessed that she felt as bad as what she wrote. We saw and focused on the strong part of her.

Luce started high school in 1988, two months short of turning fourteen. She studied hard and showed up at seven a.m. for zero-period jazz class. She had deliberately chosen to play tenor sax, an instrument usually taken by boys. I picture her playing music in our backyard in May 1989, sitting on the back of a wooden bench, one long leg extended to touch the ground, booted foot tapping the rhythm, against a backdrop of rhododendrons in full bloom. Fervor shone on her face, radiant with happiness. Surely that's not a false memory. The moment was captured on a photo, and I remember the warm lovely day around it. A cousin who visited from France had brought his own saxophone and he and Luce improvised a jazz number from a John Coltrane tune.

That same summer though, during a visit to a relative in France, Luce left the house on a very hot day to climb a cliff of unstable slick rock. There was no trail, she wore shorts, a halter-top, and flip-flops, and took no water. She was a stranger to the place and couldn't see worth a damn.

"Luce, what on earth were you thinking?" I demanded hours later. We had crisscrossed the area, driven every dirt road, walked on animal trails calling her name. The long day was dying by the time she stumbled back, having wandered aimlessly on the mountain before finding her way back. Her bare legs were bloody from falling on sharp rocks that slid under her weight, and she had twisted an ankle. She was gaunt, lips cracked and crusted. Her eyes had lost color and seemed to look at me from beyond . . . where? She could not tell from where she had returned. It seemed to me, staring into her emptied face, that it was death.

She did not think before she went to meet it. It pulled at her as she sought extreme physical risk. Several times she walked toward death and then returned. Like Persephone from the kingdom of the dead, where her lover dwelled. I remember in my adolescence sitting in the middle of the back seat on a long car trip next to a boy I thought I loved. I was too shy to be forward, but I can still feel the warm melting of muscles as I abandoned myself to the movements of the car, passively hoping for a chance contact of skin, maybe a brush of lips. Looking back, I think that Luce was in love with death at that same age. It pulled at her and she went toward it as if to her intended, but pulled back just before the embrace.

A talented young college student that I treated wrote love poems to death. She was romantic, and curiously vibrant in evoking death as if it were a young god. When I asked her to describe what she dreamt would happen after she died, she told me she pictured being accepted into a warm place of peace and beauty unimaginable in her pain-filled life. Fortunately, together, we were able to help her—first to dream of a life with such peace, beauty, and acceptance, and then to realize it.

I could not do that with my own daughter. Back then I walked in a muddle of thought and sentiment about her episodes of weird sadness and carelessness to danger. I still did not realize what we were dealing with. One hates to saddle a fourteen-year-old with a diagnosis of severe mental illness. When we met in his office, her therapist spoke of adjustment to growing up, and James and I greedily concurred: that's what we wanted. Did Luce keep her secrets to keep us happy, or could she truly not admit her despair?

The question remained to haunt me as I read more of her journal.

> It doesn't fucking matter. Nothing matters. Just Pink Floyd. Just the Final Cut. I want to blow my brains out. No reason. I just feel like it. I thought I was going to die and I wanted to. When I didn't it was just like "Oh, shit, what now?"

The new edge to her writing, the recklessness, brought back my memories of her leaving the table abruptly after dinner to shut herself in her room, and the music streaming under the door. Pink Floyd again. I hated that music.

> My head is tormenting me. I would love to just become a child of the streets—to run fast—and become hard. When I was walking down the alley last night I felt something strange. A kinship with the bricks and graffiti. I should live in those alleys and know the harsh city where I would go. This music is rushing faster and faster. In my heart I yearn to be one of those rushing dogs. I have within me a strong push to evil. The feeling I get sometimes when I'm on the streets. It's so familiar. It's been tormenting me for years. That there's something "out there."

In spite of the torment, she kept on searching for ways to live a good life, did school, drama, and music, went out with friends, and played with David and our shaggy dog. Just as I did all I knew to be a good mother to her.

Some days we met for a lunch of grilled cheese sandwiches or clam chowder at the small cafeteria on the ground floor of my office building. I took her shopping for pretty clothes on weekends. Was this ridiculously trivial in the face of her needs? Or does it count? We talked about novels, and I argued against her devotion to Ann Rice. We talked about her science classes, the faraway places she wanted to travel to, and her spiritual beliefs as she explored Buddhism. We went together, when Anna came home from New York for the summer, to a pro-choice rally where both girls shook hands with Geraldine Ferraro. We wrote letters for Amnesty International, and Luce adopted an Indonesian prisoner of conscience.

She liked to hang out at the nurses' station on weekends when I made rounds at the hospital in late afternoon. On the way home, we talked of the thrill of practicing medicine, of being so close to the heart of things. "I want your life," she said, "to be a doctor and a mom. That's just right."

I laughed at her biting impersonations of her school's office employees—"You wouldn't believe how dense that one is," she'd say, her voice thick with contempt—and I gave her tips on dealing with them courteously to get her way. We were on the same wavelength and rode the wave of our complicity.

She was also the one in the family who liked to ride sitting behind me on my Honda 250cc scooter. I love to still feel the grip of her arms around my ribs and the weight of her torso plastered against my back in the cool wind of spring as we swerved on a winding road through the hills.

Curiously, when I summon memories from those years, I don't remember James' or my own dark moods at that time. Only the worry and the love. Yet I don't doubt that our familiars were at work: my habit of self-reproach, burrowing deep and sapping my energy, or James' fits of hopeless rage around which all in the family tried to maneuver. I like to think that our worst troubles were under control by the time Luce became a teenager. James and I had certainly invested enough time and effort in psychiatric and psychological treatments over the years, as well as assorted personal growth seminars and support groups. I hadn't had a severe depression in years, and James, if not always serene, actively sought serenity.

He and I mostly agreed on how to behave with Luce since her suicide attempt. In retrospect, I see us as soldiers sharing a foxhole, relying on each other and intensely grateful not to be alone to carry the burden of responsibility.

Yet I suspect my memory is selective. Maybe I don't allow myself to recall all the times when I was depressed and he angry, in order to keep at bay my most intense regret: that I could not protect my children, those I loved most on earth, from our ingrained personal defects.

Anna is right when she says. "It's not good to be raised by a mother who is depressed." It robs children of the attention they crave and deserve, because in depression one is self-involved, self-focused, self-referential, even if the attention thus turned to the self blames, criticizes, and belittles. I have long known that anger and depression gouged desolate inner landscapes, affecting successive generations in my family as surely as fire and ice have raised and carved mountain ranges.

Such forces shaped me from the day I was born, as I learned when I presented my first-born to my mother. "It's eerie," I told Maman, who cradled Anna in her arms, "I have the feeling I'm looking at myself when I hold her." I stroked Anna's head lightly. "Did I look just like this?"

Maman raised her head, her face blank, her green eyes aimed in my direction but vague, focused behind me, as if on the past. "I don't remember what you looked like. You were like a stranger to me from the beginning." I felt a shock, yet I had known—there had always been a gulf of estrangement between us.

After she put the baby down, I asked Maman in disbelief, "Why would you say that?" We were each on one side of the bed where Anna slept, the room bright with afternoon sun. I held on tight to the crib's railing and kept my face down until I heard my mother's voice, curiously flat, unlike her.

"I couldn't look at you."

She turned her face away when I glanced up. I remained in one spot for a long time as she, emotionless, unspooled the story. "He wasn't there. Pierre. He didn't come in time, not even for this." She told me how she cried and brooded over her husband's absence, and could neither look at me nor nurse me for days.

"My mother was there. She brought you to me on the fourth day. She'd unwrapped you. You were so scrawny." She laughed a short dull chuckle. "You looked like a plucked chicken."

I stayed silent, mesmerized.

"Then she told me, 'Paula, look! Your daughter is dying. You must feed her.' And she put your mouth to my breast so I started to feed you."

She fed me but did not rejoice in my being, I thought. I drank her bitterness and despair from the first day she fed me. I couldn't move or speak. I stared at Anna's avid little mouth and noticed the weight of milk in my breasts and tears on my lashes. I wondered if Maman could ever truly see me.

By then I knew the reason for her sadness. Not long before I was conceived, she discovered that Papa was unfaithful. She had thought that after a girl and a boy, both lovely and lively, she wouldn't have more kids, but finding herself unexpectedly pregnant with me, she hoped it would at least bring my father home. That hope failed and Maman grew despondent. There was no treatment then for postpartum depression, and she took months to recover. I was bad news, I presume, all effort and no reward. We did not have a good start.

This was in 1938. France was trampled in 1940. By 1941, the Nazi invasion of France had settled into occupation. It took a while for the Germans to reach our village because it was so insignificant, hardly more than a hundred people. My father had to leave, to escape deportation to work camps in Germany where several of his cousins had already been sent. Friends hid him in their farm, tucked into a small valley close by.

When troops came to our house to requisition all the bedrooms, my mother refused to leave the house altogether. She faced the young soldiers straight on, speaking to them in her native Flemish, which they half-understood: "I will not be chased away from my own home." She spent the nights in her bedroom, door locked,

vigilant, strengthened by her righteous anger, remembering the
devastation of her first home during the previous war, when her
family had become war refugees from Belgium.

My aunt and grandmother made a makeshift sleeping room in
a small, underground root cellar for themselves and six children.
Joined mattresses on the earthen floor took up nearly the whole
place, and it felt like a nest as we slept together. I remember the
comfort of our mingled smells and the gentleness of my grandmother's voice when she spoke tender words before blowing out
the candle at night.

Papa sent word regularly that he was all right. A few times
he met Maman in a remote part of the woods, halfway between
our house and the farm where he was hidden. I am proud of my
mother: she was an icon of physical and mental courage, daring
and fortitude, the cornerstone of our lives.

Our village stood in the path of the liberating armies who
fought their way from Normandy to Paris in the summer of 1944.
When the battle was over, two German soldiers lay dead in our
courtyard and all the others had fled. We walked with our mother
out of the farm onto the road where we saw, still far away but
walking fast, my father coming back home. Papa was very thin,
his face drawn and pale, hair plastered by sweat on his brow, but
his eyes shone with joy when he saw us. We all ran to each other.
Maman cried, a rare sight, as Papa held her.

My most vivid recollections of my father took place outdoors,
in the woods or in the fields where I followed him during the
hunting season. I was never afraid in his company, in the glow
of my love for him. Looking up, I saw his thick, copper-colored
hair catch the sun's rays. Not very tall, he moved with intent and
grace, pulled by the pleasures he anticipated from the world, and
his eyes often danced with joy.

But during the slow cold years after the war, of poverty and
drabness, getting by on insufficient resources, my parents grew
tense and unhappy. Papa, disheartened by the Germans' killing
of animals he'd bred, refused to start over the research that had

satisfied his intellectual curiosity. In a town nearby, he opened a wholesale business of bath and kitchen supplies, and often did not come home at night. Maman was tortured by jealousy: she knew he did not sleep alone. I learned to keep my distance, afraid of how she struck out with words and slaps. Yet at other times she radiated pleasure, and at such moments I stepped in to bask in her warmth.

My father's presence illuminated my life like a comet in a night sky, and I mourned his absences, which increased over the years. My sister and brother married young and, in my late adolescence, the family circle of childhood was broken. Study became my refuge and I learned to rely on friends, teachers and other mentors, habits that have stood me in good stead for my whole life.

DEATH GRIP

By tenth grade Luce had filled out with long arms and legs and the high rump of an African dancer. She looked stronger in many ways, and our hope in the benefits of growing up didn't seem misplaced. She wore her thick hair short in a spiked flat top, a crown, its darkness setting off the brilliant blue of her eyes. She had been bald for most of her first year and then her hair grew straight out, not lying flat for the longest time. I see her at two, running ahead of me in the saturated Kansas light, her head in a bouncing halo of dark honey.

She cut an arresting figure at fifteen as she walked in long strides alongside her boyfriend, both of them tall, dark, and handsome in long black overcoats and Dr. Martens boots. Head held high on a long neck, full lower lip evoking a pout, unfocused gaze sliding over people, Luce appeared contemptuous to some who met her in the street. In fact, she didn't see well enough to recognize a face at a distance, but her attitude set her apart. My heart flipped at the sight of her.

One late afternoon, returning from work, I found her and David in an animated conversation in the kitchen. One glance at me and she shouted. "Run, David, run!" I caught up with them in her bedroom, tackled and tickled them on the bed.

Then I asked, "Why did you run away?"

"You had *that look*," she said. I raised hands and eyebrows in question. "When you come home, you look as if you want to kiss us all over."

Guilty as charged. I did. The love was true, the pleasure and the laughter too. One of my best memories is of a Sunday morning like many others when the kids were young. I am at the stove making crêpes. They sit on tall stools facing me across the kitchen island, inhaling the sweet, buttery smell. I listen to them comment on the past week and lazily tease each other. I slide each freshly made crêpe directly onto a plate and it is eaten right away, with a sprinkling of sugar. I look into their sleepy, joyous faces, lit by the spring sunshine coming through an east window behind me. Back then I imagined a simple life for each of them.

Only a few years later, my joy at seeing Luce was often punctured by a stab of fear. Her best friends were bright, troubled kids who discussed the meaning of life, or lack thereof, with authority and denounced society's hypocrisy with angry self-righteousness. Luce drew the anarchist A in a circle on the cover of her notebooks and pinned a poster on her bedroom wall that said "Young people should take over the world while they still know it all" or something like that. At least she hadn't lost her sense of humor. By this time, she chafed at school rules and dissed the "socies," fashionably dressed children of bourgeois families, turning her back on the social class we raised her in. She wore only black, gravitating toward oddness in grunge clothes and music. She crouched at the sides of homeless people on sidewalks to engage them in conversations. "I'm like them, really," she told me with a faraway look that weighed on me like a boulder.

Some people she befriended in recovery told hair-raising tales of their former misbehaviors with relish. I kept thinking that Luce was learning too much about life, way too soon. She selected funny snippets to make me laugh and relax, like the one of the drifter who had been dubbed Dog—I couldn't help imagining what for—and, when he acquired a dog, named him Man.

She broke up with her boyfriend after about a year because, she told us, his use of pot endangered her sobriety, and then she spent long hours alone in her room, refusing to talk about her feelings with her dad or me. The second journal we found later was written at that time. It's a black-bound ledger book, eight and a half by six inches, with "Notes" in silver letters printed on the cover and single-spaced lined pages. It looks businesslike, with entries neatly dated, mostly January through March 1991, one-third of its pages filled in a tight handwriting. But the language of those pages is the language of love and loss.

Much of it reads like any adolescent heartbreak story:

I don't miss you. I don't love you. I don't want you. I am a liar.

Except that not every sixteen-year-old considers, as Luce did in her journal, the best way to kill herself, whether by hanging from a branch in the city park close to home, or finding enough drugs to inject herself into oblivion, or standing in the middle of rush-hour traffic.

11:15 am. Is this going to be the last day of my life? I think I'll do it tonight. It's beautiful outside, really a gorgeous day. Goodbye everybody. Jesus Christ . . . I'm really going to do it, aren't I? Sorry Mom and Dad. This is kind of scary.

But then:

3 pm [the same day]. I keep stalling. For some reason I don't think I should do it, but I almost feel like forcing myself. What's holding me back is this weird instinct thing that defies logic. For some reason I'm holding on, and it almost pisses me off. I feel like telling someone I'm going to do it, just because then I'd be committed to do it. For some reason part of me doesn't want to die. My mind says "do it," and my physical body just stays put. I decided 10 hours ago that I was going to kill myself, and I'm still alive. God damn it. I don't want to just keep going on remote control. I don't want to keep on living while my brain screams "No!"

The next day:

> I have avoided killing myself for a few more hours. Why? I'm
> amazed at this will to survive. It baffles me. This instinct so innate
> and strong. It's kept me alive through mental defeat for years. I'm
> bewildered when I see how much of my life has been spent want-
> ing to die. Why don't I do it. Is it just some left over instinct or
> something more? I think I'm too scared to be a human. It takes
> a lot to live a life, and I don't think I can. I haven't told anyone
> about this. It sure would hurt my parents though.

Hardly any other mention of us in this narrative.

> I've got to get away from here,

written a little later is so tangential that it hurts. In her previous journal, three years before, she had written about being angry
with me because I made her work for me to pay for replacing a
hospital window that she had broken in anger when she was in
the adolescent unit. And she had complained of her father telling
her one moment she was great, smart, and good, and then yell-
ing that she was irresponsible, spoiled, and mean for disrespecting
him. But we were absent from the second journal. Only one entry
concerned her therapist:

> I could become a twelve-step god with 20 years sober at 33. I could
> kill myself tomorrow. Live to be a doctor. A super junkie on death
> row. Who cares? Matt [her therapist] does. Matt really does. I don't
> know why.

I am pained that we, the adults appointed to help, appear so useless. But I also feel a guilty relief at not being shown as a bad guy.
Mean little comfort.
    There are frequent appeals to God, the higher power she want-
ed to rely on.

God, grant me the strength to forgive. Grant me the strength to love. Grant me the strength to look outside and see a beautiful day. Please, God, help me along the way. Help me clear a place for you in my heart.

On page after page, begging, hoping, praying, she used the same religious words I had used in my youth to ward off despair. But toward the end she wrote.

I could bail. Start using and head to California. No love. No God. You're only 16, things could get better. Maybe I'll find solace there. "I'm a child of God." Fuck, man, it was just chance. Live for Beauty? I don't think so. Live to be in service? Hell, I only carry the mess. I'm a fucking spiritual reject.

One evening in that spring of 1991, her junior year—I realize that it could have been soon after she wrote this last quote in the black notebook—Luce stood up to put away her dinner dishes, then turned with a casual look at her father and me. "I'm getting out of school. It's so lame, I can't stand it anymore."

"What are you talking about?" James asked her, pushing his chair back, the muscles on his lean arms knotted as he gripped the edge of the table with both hands.

"Jazz band is the only good thing there and I had to quit." Her lips pinched as if not to cry, and she shook her head like a soaked dog getting rid of water. "I can't read the damned partition when I stand." She hammered the words. "My eyes are too bad."

"We can get you new glasses," I said in my usual infuriatingly reasonable voice.

"No, Mom," she shouted. "That's not it. I want to travel, go see the world." Her irritation was promptly replaced by a smile. "It will be good practice for when I am with Doctors Without Borders." She knew I melted whenever she mentioned her plans to be a doctor.

"What would you live on?" James' face was tight.

She looked down at her father with contempt as if his only concern was money. She stood erect, feet apart and arms crossed, her face severe. "Don't worry, I'll support myself. I'll find a job."

"Luce, that's crazy!" I thumped my fist on the table in frustration. "You're sixteen, you can't even get a good enough job that's legal. You're young, you're gorgeous, and you believe every weirdo's story. Don't you see what will happen to you?"

"No, no." She didn't sound argumentative, more sweetly seductive now, a tinge of condescension in her reassuring tone. "I'll be okay, Mom. Don't worry. I can take care of myself."

James and I had the good sense to stop arguing at that point and ask for time to think, which she granted us with a regal wave of her hand before going to her room.

We were frightened of course, and, in the following days, used all our influence to keep her involved in school until we could devise a plan of action. Luce agreed, adding, "Not for long," with an insistent stare. We couldn't ignore what she said. This was a kid who, at two, regularly left the house in the middle of the night in her little pink nightgown to explore the neighborhood, and we didn't even know it for weeks. Not until one night when James bolted the back door, which usually remained unlocked, and she had to ring the front door bell at 2 a.m.

From the time Luce could walk, she had gone her own way in shopping malls and office buildings—without particular malice, but without warning. Once, at the Saint Louis airport on the way back from vacation when she was three, she looked out the window at a blizzard and left without a word to find a plane to "go back to the beach," she said later in all innocence, surprised that we were so upset after searching for her for almost an hour. Then there was the time when, inspired by watching *Peter Pan*, she flew off our high porch railing and landed in bushes, scratched and bruised, but not broken. We'd had to throw away the tape of the movie.

Curiosity propelled her, and we could not instill enough fear in her to keep her close. It was one of the traits that I, and many others, loved, but it was exhausting to watch over her. James often said, "If we lived in the wilderness of ancient times, this child would be dead. She would have strayed from the fire and been eaten by a tiger."

So we talked and talked to her, trying to enlist her intelligence and reason to plan her future. She was already taking advanced placement science classes, and we suggested that she do more of that.

"No. High school is stupid, I want out. Mom, you got out of high school at sixteen. Why can't I?"

I pointed out that I had graduated with my class, not dropped out, and that she'd be penalized for quitting, that it would be harder to enter a good university with a GED.

Then James remembered, from his own graduate studies in education, that high school graduation was not an absolute requirement for admission to college. In desperation, he told Luce that she could petition our state university for early admission. It would be a difficult process to be granted special dispensation. She'd need recommendations from her high school teachers and to be interviewed by university administrators. We struck a bargain: we still preferred that she complete high school with her peers, but if she got accepted at the university we would support her.

Teachers whom she asked for references called James. "You must stop pushing that child. It's irresponsible." He heard the unspoken question: "What's wrong with you?" He tried to explain that, far from pushing, we were hanging on for dear life as on a skiff in a gale wind, and only trying to steer her in a better direction.

Looking back on that time, the hardest thing to do is recapture how dense my "not-knowing" was. From today's vantage point, it is hard—no, impossible—to ignore what would be revealed a few months later in the full-blown manifestation of Luce's manic-depressive illness. I want to flog myself for not considering what seems so plain in hindsight: her excessive confidence, single-minded purpose, intense energy, and powers of persuasion could indicate a manic episode. Why didn't they raise my suspicions?

Some psychiatrist! Or was I, her mother, just too tempted to welcome her new bright optimism, focus, and appetite for life after
years of confusing doubt. Even though she had protected us by not
spelling out the depths of her suffering and despair nor sharing
the details of her obsession with death, fear and uncertainty had
oozed from her. I can understand that I would have done anything to leave behind the haunting images of the hollow-cheeked,
narrow-shouldered, hunkering thirteen-year-old who watched
horror movies. But the guilt of failing my own child swells up in
me like a flooding river, dirty and cold, hauling dangerous debris.
Who knows if the course of her illness might have been less severe
if medication treatment had begun sooner? Not I, possibly no one
else either.

Missing the full picture did not stop us from acting on her
behalf as best we could. I write *we* because James and I were united in our love for our daughter and our intent to help her. Like
her, we could be misguided but courageous. I am frightened to
recognize how often in my life I did passionately dedicate considerable resources of intelligence, heart, and will to the service of
a poor decision, based on bad information or bad judgment. The
fact that I am not alone offers scant solace. I can only humbly
remember the fog of uncertainty.

The pursuit of early admission to the university channeled Luce's
energies and focused her on doing well in classes. And she succeeded. She was allowed to start at the university in September
1991, two months before her seventeenth birthday.

She went to the senior prom with two girlfriends, none of them
bothering with dates. She wore a clingy, long velvet dress, bright
lipstick on her happy mouth, and came back drenched in sweat
from dancing all night.

After the end of school, Luce convinced us that she should practice living away from home. For a month she shared an apartment
by the university with a friend, found a small job and shadowed—
the word used in medical school—two of my colleagues, a general
surgeon and a neurosurgeon, in their hospital duties to gather

some inside knowledge of what they actually did. Dropping by her apartment one Saturday, I wasn't happy to find the girls asleep way past noon and the place a mess of clothes, melted candles, and fast-food containers, the smell of yesterday's grease mixed with Indian incense. But Luce soon distracted me over pizza at the restaurant next door by telling stories of fractured bones being fixed in the emergency ward and of the sound of a drill piercing through skull in the operating room. "These women, they are so strong. They keep on working for hours. That's definitely what I want to be."

She met Josh that summer. He was nineteen, short, blond, moody, and quiet, and had just moved from a tiny town in the country to work in his father's service station. Gentle and generous, indulged by his mother and older sisters, he was bowled over by Luce, he said, by her beauty and her brains, and wanted to marry her. They talked about having a baby, scaring us all over again.

But our three weeks of vacation in France were good. We made the rounds of aunts, cousins, and friends. Anna and Luce were familiar with my family. Being French as well as US citizens, they had been able to attend for a month at a time the one-room public school in the village where I grew up and my mother still lived. Maman's death, occurring before David was old enough to stay with her by himself, had prevented him from learning French like his sisters, and he was bored sitting at the edge of long conversations. So James took David bicycling for a week, and in the process discovered that he himself loved riding on the narrow roads that go from one old village to another.

The last three entries in Luce's journal of that year have a different tone than the earlier ones, less frantic, more reflective. In August, she mentions rereading the diary and notes,

> If I really am good and innocent, how I've been feeling is so sad.

I agree with her, she didn't deserve such torment and I too am sad. I want to gather her up in my arms to kiss the pain I couldn't take away.

> 8-21-91. Isn't life strange? An awful lot like climbing a mountain. Young kids are just the embodiments of potential. Raw, unadulterated opportunity. Obscure. I'm very fast becoming an adult. It's a sad feeling. Feel kind of stuck. Trapped, hooked into a rail. I'm swimming in my own blindness, drowning. If I don't learn to swim, to get to shore, I'll be inexorably coaxed into apathy thru ignorance to my own condition, usually final and fatal.

Here is her last paragraph, on the day she moved out of our home to start college.

> 9-4-91. Well here I am, on my way. I'm going to miss France. This was the first time I was there that I really was interested in the people. Starting school again. Am I going to make it. Will I completely fail. No, of course not, but I could if I'm not careful. I'll study my ass off.

These last words she wrote in the journal are not what stunned me when I looked at that page. At the top I saw my own handwriting. "Good luck, ta Maman qui t'aime, Elsa," with a heart and three xxx kisses. So I knew of the journal. It had to be on Luce's desk that day before she wrote her last entry on the same page. We even used the same pen, and I imagine that this pen held the blank page open on that day and I took it to write my well-wishing words.

I am certain that I didn't read what she'd written in the previous pages of her journal until it was found much, much later. Should I have read it, gathered the information it held? Would it have made a difference? I wonder of course, yet I can't even wish I had. It would have been unthinkable to break our family's agreement about privacy. I would have had to be a different person.

When university classes began, Luce settled into an apartment close to the university, a studio on the second floor of an ordinary, drab, concrete building. She particularly enjoyed philosophy and chemistry. She was inspired, she said, and loved that her mind was thoroughly engaged. She seemed happy.

David began ninth grade, Anna was in her third year at New York University. James and I were ready to relax.

On the evening of October 15, 1991, days away from her seventeenth birthday, Luce walked from Josh's nearby place back to hers, intent on homework. In the very short time it took to walk five blocks, she was seized by the absolute conviction that she must kill herself. She was certain it was ordained, that she had no choice but to decide how she would die. There had been no provoking event, no reason. She didn't need a reason, that's just how it was, she told me later, matter-of-factly.

She walked a block past her apartment building to a busy boulevard, surveyed the intense traffic, and considered how to throw herself under the wheels of a heavy, speeding truck. Two thoughts stopped her, she later explained. She knew, after watching the trauma surgeon she had shadowed two months before, that she might not die, and she thought that the driver of the truck would be blamed, his life maybe ruined.

Back at her place, she considered tying a plastic bag over her head, but instead looked in her belongings for an electric cord, something she had long ago thought she could use to hang herself.

Then she remembered Josh, whom she had just left. She couldn't bear to have him blame himself, so she called him. "Josh, I've decided to kill myself. It's not your fault. I just have to do this. I love you." And hung up. Josh was stunned. Bless him, he called our number. "I'll go right away," I told him. "Meet me there." I can't remember where James or David were at that time—just not at home.

It took me five minutes to reach her place. I drove tight with fear, fighting off visions of slashes and blood. I parked at the bottom of the stairs and rushed up, banged on the door of Luce's apartment, called her name. No answer, but a bar of light under the door gave me hope that she was in. I pressed the whole front of my body against the hard door as if that could help me sense what was happening on the other side, and forced my breathing to quiet as I put an ear to the wood. I heard noises, indistinct rustlings. No voice, but no moans either. So there was movement, that was good. I called again, knocked some more, still without answer.

The corridor was dark and the other three apartments seemed unoccupied, without light or sound. I would have liked someone to help, I didn't know how, but at the same time I was happy for the quiet. I didn't want to explain that my daughter was maybe in the process of killing herself in there. Shame undergirded my worry. Alone, for better and for worse, I had to find a way to reach her.

I walked to the end of the corridor and saw a balcony in front of her living room sliding door. I climbed over railings to step onto the balcony and tried to see inside the apartment. The curtains were drawn, but light shone through and that encouraged me. I called Luce's name again, pleading with her to let me in. The silence rendered me frantic. I pushed and pulled, trying to pry open the sliding panes until one gave a bit. I remember being grateful for the building's shoddy construction when the aluminum frame started bending. I concentrated on the latch area. I used hands, shoulders, feet, in tears but with strength quadrupled by determination. I was finally able to partially open the door and squeeze through.

Parting the drapes, I saw Luce in the middle of the room, alive, but my relief was brief because I couldn't figure what she was doing. She seemed not to know I was there. She stood on a stool, an electric cord around her neck, fiddling with the overhead light fixture. I'd later find out that she had already tried to hang herself, but the part to which she'd tied the cord tore loose when she kicked the stool. With plaster on her hair and shoulders, she was now threading the cord directly through the ceiling hook. She did not respond when I called her name, as if she did not hear me. I wrapped my arms around her legs, held them tight, ready to support her weight if she let go. I moaned but held on for what seemed an eternity. She was tense in my grip, still raised toward the ceiling.

Finally, I felt a hand fall on my head, her weight relax against my shoulder. The cord slid down. I brought my daughter down into my arms and we both sat huddled on the floor, rocking. "I want to die, I want to die," she chanted softly. She seemed so far away. I hung on to her, kissed her cheeks, brushed plaster off her hair.

Josh knocked at the door then, calling Luce's name. It had taken him a long time before he could move after her telephone call because he was too spooked to do anything besides call me. He'd finally talked to a friend and found the courage to walk over to Luce's. I let him in. His face was pale under his short blond hair, his eyes questioning.

I went back to Luce, pulling her slowly to her feet. "Come," my voice soft, enticing, "we'll take you to the hospital."

"No," was all she said, softly. "No," not looking at me but backing away in slow motion.

I nodded to Josh who joined me, and we held her gently by each arm. Head down, she shuffled vaguely as we urged her forward. We propped her up to walk down the stairs. I sat them in the back of my car, asking Josh to hold her tight, locked the doors from inside, and drove toward the hospital. When Luce recognized the building, she tried to free herself from Josh's embrace to reach the door handle. He held her, panic in his eyes. I watched in the rearview mirror, afraid she'd rush into traffic, immensely grateful to him. Fortunately, she seemed distracted, unfocused, not determined or strong in her struggle.

I pulled right up to the entrance of the psychiatric ward and led Luce by the hand to the nurse's station where she had accompanied me many a time. She didn't seem to recognize the place or the people. But the sight of familiar faces comforted me and relief drained some of the tension from my shoulders.

Luce was alive and professionals I trusted would help me take care of her. I was not at that moment aware of my hope that their friendly regard for me might reduce the chance that I would be summarily judged and shamed, but that contributed to my relief. Any parent called in to the principal's office or the police head-quarters knows what I'm talking about.

The admitting doctor guided us to an office. Luce had not spo-ken or looked up, and let me hold her limp hand to lead her. We sat in metal chairs in front of the plain desk, a yellow pad the only color in the room, night darkening the windows behind the doctor. He and I nodded to each other in recognition and got on with the business at hand. I gave an account of the last hour: Josh's call, the near hanging, the drive, in a few words that sounded surprisingly reasonable to my own ears. I mentioned the dates of her hospitali-zation at thirteen, the name of her therapist, her recent admission at the university, and her move away from home. The psychiatrist wrote it all down, then said he wanted to speak to her alone.

Once back in the waiting room where Josh sat slumped in the corner of a couch, I went to hug him. He leaned against me like a child. "Thank you for calling me," I said. "She's safe now." He just nodded. "Will you be okay to go home," I asked, "do you have a friend who can stay with you?"

"I'll call my mom." He left with the promise that I'd call him the next day.

Then I phoned home. James' resonant voice filled the handset. "I wondered where you were. Were you called to the hospital?"

"Well . . . yes. But not for a patient. I just brought Luce in."

"What's wrong?" James' voice had lost all luster.

I answered in a hush, as if I didn't want him to hear the words. "She tried to kill herself."

A silence, then he asked, "What'd she do?"

I told him in a few sentences and heard "Oh no" in a strangled, high-pitched scream. Then "Where is she? I'll come" between sobs.

I was finally crying too. "No, it's too late for visitors tonight. She's safe, we can come in the morning." He was still sobbing when I said, "I'm coming home right away," before hanging up.

We huddled for a long time on our living room couch—James, David, and I—in silence, unable to move, not wanting to go to bed, long after the last words had been said, the last details gone over. We were left with only questions, no answers.

That night, Luce was put in a locked room with an attendant present at all times because she tried to flee as soon as she was left alone. Staff told us the next day that she did not speak, only paced. At the change of nursing shifts, she went quietly to the farthest corner of the room, looped the belt of her hospital robe around her neck, attached the end to a window handle, and let herself slide along the wall to tighten the noose, keeping her face hidden. The new nurse rushed when she saw Luce's body jerk, unconscious.

They resuscitated her, gave her oxygen, but the capillaries of her face had all broken from the pressure of the belt around her neck. She bore for days the purple stigmata of her suffering. When asked for her reasons, she repeated with a shrug of the shoulders and an exasperated sigh that she had to die, that's all. Her conviction was so absolute that, when pressed, she insisted she could not understand why the staff, and her parents, did not agree with her, why we did not accept that she knew what she was doing, and what must be done. "I'm supposed to be dead," with emphasis on *supposed*, was all the explanation she could give.

I had for many years witnessed in my patients the pull of the suicidal impulse, driven by what is called a mood-congruent delusion, the mark of severe depression, inaccessible to rational debate: the unchallenged certainty that one's death—at this time—is ordained.

The most astonishing example for me came from a patient I had treated for a long time in the hospital. A short, middle-aged woman, she was only remarkable by her stubborn dedication to kill herself. Her attempts had been repeatedly thwarted by the staff's vigilance, yet she tried again and again in spite of all the therapeutic interventions we could bring to bear. One day she told me, "Nobody will be able to stop me, you know. I will do it."

The next morning she was found dead in her bed and the autopsy could not identify a specific cause. All we could imagine was that, as incomprehensible as it was, she had finally willed herself to die.

Each of us carries powers of destruction, unequal in force from one person to the next, from one moment to another. On the evening of October 15, 1991, Luce's enemy revealed its awesome power. No longer could she keep it at bay. She accepted it, agreed that she must die.

I recognized the death instinct. It had almost killed me as well.

THE ENEMY WITHIN

I was twenty-six then, fresh from medical school, in private practice for a year as a general practitioner and unable to make a go of it. Too few patients straggled in: teenage girls who came to see the only woman doctor in the provincial French town in which I lived, new mothers who had noticed that their infants were not afraid of my young face, and some curious neighbors. Until this time, all I had needed to succeed was hard work. But now I was helpless, utterly confused and humiliated that, at the end of every month, I had to borrow from my father to pay the mortgage.

I'd looked for more work. Doctors in private practice took turns being on call for admissions at the small local hospital, and I spread the word around that I'd be happy to take over my colleagues' call duties. I ended up spending several nights a week at the hospital, and still sat all day in my office. Sleeplessness added exhaustion to the mix of my troubles, yet I never even considered that I might suffer from depression and need treatment. My life was unraveling, financial, physical, and emotional resources leaking from me. Worry accompanied my obsessive thoughts about work and money, and wounded pride stopped me from asking for help.

One late December afternoon, a patient came to complain about me, explaining how I had treated her badly, then left before

I could make amends. She slammed the door, leaving me acutely ashamed. I don't remember thinking. I don't remember crying or sitting to ponder the situation. A surge of unyielding resolve pushed me away from the door, away from the outside world, toward the room at the back of my office. I faced the cabinet where medication samples were stored, and opened it to survey the bright cardboard boxes, neatly ordered by category. Clear-eyed and coldhearted, I chose every single packet of barbiturates that was there, put them on the gleaming tiled counter by the sink, and extracted every sleeping pill. I washed them down fastidiously with glass after glass of water, swallowing slowly so as not to throw up. Then I turned off the lights, locked the door, went to my apartment, and lay on my bed in the waning light of day.

As I look back, I see how incendiary shame, fueled by guilt, led to an immediate and drastic condemnation. No more than a half hour from the time I saw and accepted the judgment in the woman's eyes, I had decreed that I deserved capital punishment, swallowed the poison, and closed my eyes for what I believed was immediate death. The suicidal impulse fell upon me like the blade of a guillotine.

As it would many years later for Luce.

But after some time, through my drowsiness, I remembered that a friend had invited me to dinner that evening. Good manners saved my life, just as Luce's call to Josh would save hers when she was seventeen. I dialed my friend's number from the bedside phone to excuse myself. She heard the thickness of my slowed voice and tried to get a story that I could no longer articulate. By the time she banged on my door, I could not hear or respond, so she called the manager who came with his passkey. An ambulance took me to the ICU in Paris.

When I came to, I felt the strong pull of nothingness. Nothingness, stronger than any sleep. I wasn't supposed to wake up. Confusion overwhelmed me and I drifted again until a nurse came into the room.

"Five days!" I exclaimed when she answered my questions about what I was doing there. "But I don't remember."

"You've been in a coma. You talked sometimes, but I guess you were not totally back." She sounded matter-of-fact. "How do you feel?"

I stared at her, mystified. The last I remembered, I was certain I'd soon die, and here I was. How was I supposed to feel? I'd missed, failed. I was mad. But I couldn't say that, ashamed of having tried to kill myself and ashamed of having failed, so I turned my head to the wall and shut my eyes and mind, hoping to go away into sleep if she didn't leave first.

I didn't know then that major depression strikes about one in ten women every year. According to US public health data, among adults experiencing a major depressive episode, fifty-six percent thought that it would be better if they were dead, forty percent considered suicide, fifteen percent made a plan, and ten percent an attempt. Suicide is the eleventh leading cause of death among adults and accounts for well over thirty thousand deaths per year.

I would learn only later that what we now call bipolar and unipolar major depressive disorders had surfaced with regularity in my family for several generations.

On the ninth day of my hospital stay, a doctor checked my medical condition, concluded that I'd have no permanent damage—physically that is—and gave me the name of a psychiatrist whom I should go see after discharge. But I didn't make the appointment.

My logic, shared with no one, was that I should seek treatment only if I wanted to get better. So I first had to decide whether I wanted to live or not. I realized that neither of the contradictory acts—first swallowing the barbiturates, then making the phone call before I lost consciousness—had been rationally decided. That left me to contemplate the tremendous force field within me of opposite drives that, instead of canceling each other, tugged me toward irreconcilable outcomes. The only thing to do then was withhold action until I knew more. How would I know? No idea. But I would try to hold still until clarity came so as not to capsize.

A path did gradually become clear. If death reached out

arbitrarily, I saw that I could only live by accepting that life was capricious, my mind unclear, emotions painful, and certainties a lure. And by having the courage to go forward as an explorer, so intent on discovery that I would not crouch in fear when bad things happened.

I made a contract with myself that still holds: not to kill myself, even piecemeal, even if suicidal. Then, at last, I began psychotherapy. I obtained a degree in statistics applied to medicine and found work in a research lab, which allowed me to regain a sense of professional competence.

It took many years to feel secure that the tools I acquired would pull me through hardships. I faltered at times, but never reconsidered my resolve to choose life, in spite of its chaotic ups and downs.

By 1991 I thought that my resolve had been amply tested. But nothing had prepared me for facing Luce, who herself lacked neither curiosity nor courage, with the imprint of the cord around her neck and broken capillaries all over her face.

QUICKSAND

This couldn't be Luce, I thought, when a nurse escorted her into the waiting room where James and I sat in oppressed silence. Not the girl who only a few days before had told us she was inspired by her classes. Gone the bounce in her step, the shine in her eyes, the smile all at once ironic and joyous. I stood still, unable to move toward this person whom I hardly recognized. She looked like a shuffling old woman with a puffy, discolored face and matted hair, or a child, holding the nurse's hand as if she couldn't figure how to walk to us.

James took her in his arms, murmuring words I didn't hear. I went and held her hand. She hung her head and tears made their slow way down her cheeks. I dared not wipe them, afraid to hurt her poor face. "Sorry," she said, in a whisper. We three huddled for a long moment, united in sorrow.

Our local psychiatric ward was meant for short-term treatment of adult patients and not equipped to deal with such a severe case in so young a girl as Luce, who wasn't yet seventeen. The staff arranged for transfer by ambulance to a child and adolescent unit at a major hospital, two hours away. For the next month James and I, sometimes together, sometimes separately, drove up several times a week to the massive hospital complex.

Pressing the doorbell to seek admission to the fifth floor

{ 57 }

psychiatric unit released a jet of dread in my guts every time I came. The bunker-feel of locked doors and windowless security rooms underscored the danger Luce was in, and the tense expression of the nurses and social worker I met showed that her treatment was not easy. For several weeks she kept a frigid distance, barely answered the therapists' questions, and, when she did, used big words as if she were a bored peer and not the haunted kid they saw. She refused to participate in group activities, made snooty comments about parlor games, ate a minimum, and wanted cigarettes the staff told her she was too young to have. As if compelled to make up for my daughter's bad manners, I smiled at the other patients in the common room, exuded goodwill toward the staff, and gave them every bit of information they asked for. Facing Luce, still dressed only in black grungy clothes although we'd brought prettier ones from home, I tried hard not to show the fear gripping me. Her eyes were cold and opaque.

Even more painful than the arrival, the last quick embrace of my daughter and the catch of the lock behind me when I exited the unit left me weak with apprehension. How would she be until next time? I had to seek a bench in an anonymous corridor and close my eyes, hearing carpet-muted footsteps around me and disembodied calls for doctors on the loudspeakers, and wait until the tears had come and gone before I could get in the car for the long drive home. If we were together, James and I often remained silent all the way back.

David, then close to his fourteenth birthday, came twice with us to visit Luce and met once alone with a family therapist and his sister. He hated to be there. The ward scared him with its locked doors and kids his age hanging out, defeated, in the halls. Luce spooked him, sickly thin, not looking at or speaking to him, a scowl on her face instead of the tender, teasing smile she usually reserved for him.

One morning early in Luce's second week there, James and I were ushered into a meeting room adjacent to the nurses' station to join the treatment team. We sat close to the wall in back, and I stared through the tall window at the other end of the long narrow

room, surprised that so much clear light streamed through in late
October. I felt light-years away from the familiar scene as staff
filed in, greeted each other, and placed coffee cups and papers on
the long narrow table before taking a seat. My brain swimming in
confusion, I strained to focus.

Each staff member spoke in turn to report on the physical and
neurological evaluations, lab results, nurses' observations, psychological testing, and family assessment. Some seemed hesitant at
first, sliding glances at James and me. But the psychiatrist, author-
itative and smart, took charge, asking questions and requesting
opinions, so that the attention soon focused on her. She contributed her own findings from interviews with Luce and led a discussion on what was wrong and what needed to be done. I fixed my
gaze on her. She was about forty with curly black hair and intense
eyes. I was comforted that she seemed to like Luce. James and I
held hands under the table, our shoulders touching as we leaned a
little toward each other, both looking straight ahead.

There was no brain damage, no tumor, no drug or alcohol use,
no physical reason for the symptoms. Luce was still in a delusional
state, focused on self-destruction. She was suicidal, hardly eating,
and barely noticing other people unless spoken to. All tests and
observations pointed to a severe form of bipolar illness. She was
not yet any better, although she had been on appropriate doses of
lithium and antidepressants for more than ten days.

I understood all too well the implications of what I heard: the
enormous burden of a lifelong disabling illness, the high risk of
death by suicide. I stood when the others did but stayed immobile, as if rooted in place, shaky from helplessness and dread, while
James walked to the door. The psychiatrist came to me, put firm
hands gently on my shoulders, and looked at me straight. "We'll
do all we can," she said. "But you are her mother. As long as she is
alive you can't give up." I nodded, looking at her through my tears,
then moved ahead. There was a comfort in simply being needed,
possibly useful.

I only thought of requesting medical records from Luce's hospital stays when I began writing about her. I also thought such records would be of value to Anna, David, and their families to come.

Difficult reading, like plunging back into turbulent waters when I thought I had made it safely to the bank of the river, just as the reading of Luce's diaries had been. What was I looking for? I don't exactly know.

First, the corroboration of my memories reassured me that I had been a correct historian. More precious, mentions within the hospital files of Luce's appearance and behavior brought her back as she was then, in the way that a photograph would have.

The psychologist's attempt at fine-grained renditions of her inner world fascinated me. He described what we knew well: how her high innate abilities would be rendered inoperative by the assault of hurricane-force emotions and bizarre thinking.

> Abrupt shifts in mood and sudden impulses to discharge tension . . . Interesting contrast between feeling alone, bleak and passive, and actively playing dangerous games with malevolent external forces . . . She seems intent on taunting whatever distresses her. It's as though Luce is trying to prove to herself that she can survive the onslaught and triumph over the adversity.

This summoned an image of the day when she had stumbled back, bloodied and parched, from the cliff in France. Also her announcement, at sixteen, that she'd take to the road on her own. And I thought of the demons she told me she'd encountered in the desert.

Most troubling were the family therapist's sharply observed and well-written descriptions of James and me. I am accustomed to being the seer, the observer. Reading his notes, I saw myself being seen, our family's inner workings revealed.

An entire movie came to my mind, vividly reeled in an instant. L'Arroseur Arrosé, the first narrative film made in France in 1895, lasts one minute. A gardener deploys a long hose and ambles through his vegetable patch, watering. When the water stops, he first shakes the nozzle with a puzzled frown. At that point, we see what he cannot see: a boy, hidden from the gardener by a bush, has placed his foot on the hose. His shoulders shake with a silent cackle as he watches the man pick up the hose and look into the nozzle. When the boy lifts his foot off the hose, a gush of water drenches the gardener. He is, as the title states, the waterer watered. Reading the family therapy notes, I was the observer observed, similarly drenched by cold rushing awareness.

The account of one particular family meeting chilled me. We had been ushered into an undecorated room, too large for four persons, with a bank of windows letting in the dulled light of an overcast sky high above the city. The therapist, a young man built like a marathon runner, took a seat, placing the ubiquitous yellow notepad at his right on the wide arm of the chair. We filed in to sit across from him. I chose the corner of a wide Naugahyde-covered couch, Luce passed me to settle in a single chair farther away, and James sat at the other end of the couch.

The notes read, after an introductory paragraph:

The focus turned to the father stating that he could no longer support Luce living alone and himself paying for it. Although the father's words were certainly caring, they had a sharp bite to them. Luce appearing to react more to the father's tone than his words, angrily stated that she could not live with him and move back home. I interpreted to Mr. Keane that although his words came from a loving, caring place, they indeed sounded angry and incongruent. The father then exploded into what, for the family, can only be described as a terrifying outburst. With a booming voice he shouted that he never wanted to be pulled into family therapy. His anger quickly turned to the mother and he ragefully began to attack her for a conflict over last night's dinner, that reignited during the car ride to the hospital this morning. During this interchange Luce's affect turned to sobbing tears with her head turning from side to side as if she was trying to fend off her painful feelings. She then turned her head to me with a tearful expression as if to say, "You see."

Mother's face became contorted with pain and she reached across the couch to the father who immediately jumped to the other side stating, "Don't touch me. I want to be alone." He then turned to the mother in a loud vitriolic tone stating, "You always have to have the last word, you attack me for not working. You've been doing it for years." It was as if with each rageful sentence Mr. Campion seemed to lose additional boundaries. His voice at this point was literally booming off the walls creating fear in both Luce and the mother. Luce continued to sob stating with her head shaking, "I can't live there, I can't live there, I can't live there."

As Mr. Keane's composure began to return during a guarded truce he stated, "I've had to take care of myself since I was 2-years-old, I've had to act like this." The therapist's response was to state that although it made sense to act that way when he was 2-years-old, it doesn't make any sense now and only ends up terrifying family members.

Of course I remember how James would explode, fly apart like a grenade, how his words became projectiles. But what stunned me when I read the notes was that I looked only at James and didn't turn back to look at my daughter, crushed by the blast. And that I reached out to touch him instead of standing up to get away from the onslaught and assist Luce. As if there were no other option.

Intellectually, I understand that being raised by an explosive mother, whose attacks I was too little to avoid, could be like a yoga practice, teaching me to hold unnatural positions for an inordinate length of time. But if someone screams, it doesn't make sense to go toward him to reason and soothe instead of backing off. I thought that, by then, I'd stopped trying to appease unreasonable people, and it shames and saddens me that I hadn't, because my response imposed an additional burden on my children, who were left alone with their fear.

Notes from the following week's meeting read:

Father brought up the issue of his angry outburst, and is open to the family dealing with him in a different way. Mother feels her response has been irrational, and is determined to no longer give him nurture when he is experiencing his "survival response."

When mother discussed commitment to future family therapy, both father and Luce lapsed into a look of deep despair. When asked, both told me their expectations were minimal, but that they would "go along with it."

I so much wanted help from others, for Luce's sake, for all of us. Diminished by fear in front of the huge challenge of her illness, I couldn't see how we'd make it on our own. I needed someone who believed in hope.

A couple of weeks before, the family therapist had invited James to his office to meet with Luce without the rest of the family. The therapist wrote,

> Luce told her father that, as a child, she felt afraid and hurt by his anger. She stated that his anger communicated to her that she was a self-serving child who really didn't care about others. She recalled her father saying, in the past, "If I was laying somewhere bleeding, nobody in this family would care."

James had his own demons to contend with, survivors from his childhood or brought forth by alcoholism and the bouts of severe depression that overpowered him every few years, even in sobriety. But his relationship with Luce was further complicated by the similarities they took pleasure in. They often noted that they read people and situations the same way and spoke, without forethought, the very same words at the same time. This closeness made of shared thoughts and experiences, including, but greater than addiction and recovery, pleased both of them. I have under my eyes a note Luce wrote during her adolescence: "Dear Dad, there is nobody I'd like better to have as a father than you."

I know that James strove to be a good person and a giving father, and that his intentions were true. To my mind and his children's, that counts even if unpredictable anger got the better of him all too often.

My own shortcomings are clear in the family therapist's notes of the session when David and Luce were alone with him.

> David says in a soft, barely audible voice, that he has a close relationship with his father, sharing many activities like skiing, biking, and conversations. David describes his anger primarily at his mother who, he states, does not listen, is often preoccupied and has a tendency to repeat herself over and over, even after David has responded.

In those years, my reluctant son considered "I don't know," "Fine," and a shrug, adequate responses to my inquiries about homework or his feelings.

Another entry from the same day reads:

> Luce stated that she had to keep rejecting mother's attempts to care for her emotionally because she had to salvage her sense of self, in response to mother's intrusiveness.

Reading all this brought back my greatest quandary about being a mother: how much talking and questioning is too much? It also revived a pained awareness of the many ways one can hurt tender children, and the ways I've hurt mine. By not looking at my anguished daughter, for example, or not listening to my lonely son.

The family therapist continued:

> Luce shared a childhood dream, where she is in a hospital, being operated on, and on anesthesia. In the dream, her entire family comes to rescue her, and ends up drowning in quicksand.

Luce is not responsible for this, but at the time, I feared our family was about to drown in the quicksand of helplessness and despair. It would take all the energy we had to resist the pull.

So, when Luce was discharged after four weeks, we each did what we were told would help. One foot in front of the other, slow and stubborn. Luce lived with us, took her medications, and James drove her to appointments with a local psychiatrist or to the lab for lithium serum levels. Dinners at home were quiet, restful after the intense stirrings when Luce was in the hospital. In the evenings, she read *The Mists of Avalon* by the fire in the living room, feet tucked under her and a caressing hand on the tummy of the cat who stretched his spine along her thigh. Anna called regularly from New York to check in with her.

I went to work, grateful that my practice was well-established and functioned smoothly thanks to my efficient secretary, whose gentle manner reassured patients. Twenty years of experience served me well in focusing on my patients and I received wonderful support from my colleagues, who'd covered for me on the days I went to visit Luce in the hospital. I met regularly with one of them in peer supervision, warmed by our brotherly closeness and stimulated by the intellectual challenge of discussing difficult cases.

Working gave me stability and self-confidence. I followed many patients with the same illnesses that plagued many members of my family. When those patients took a turn for the worse, it scared me, but more often I was buoyed by the progress of those patients who made impressive gains, and was proud to have contributed to it.

I also appreciated that my income took care of my family's needs. Because I was self-employed in solo practice and James hadn't been a teacher in many years, we did not have group health insurance. Individual policies did not reimburse the cost of drug and alcohol rehab, nor the treatment of mental illness—except for short-term hospitalization—making a scientifically unfounded and glaringly unfair difference between *physical* and *mental* illnesses. As if we were not whole beings, but rather masses of noncommunicating parts. In the state where I practiced for many years, the rule was only changed on January 1, 2007 after decades of lobbying by mental health advocates on behalf of patients often too ill to campaign for their own rights. Over Luce's teens in the early 1990s, we paid an average of 24,000 dollars a year on her care, for therapists, doctors, labs, and medicines—the cost of the medical school Luce had hoped to attend.

David did his part to help as well. He went to school and turned in his homework, kept the volume of his heavy metal music low, and took the dog for long walks without being reminded. We all worked as a unit, cleared of disagreements by our common concern, gentled by sorrow, fostering each other's hopes.

One evening, David brought Kohl, a long-haired mix of Australian shepherd and collie, in the house to say good-night. She fixed her dark-lined eyes on the kids in adoration and licked their faces, bringing on one of Luce's rare smiles. "I can't believe," she said, brushing the dreadlocks that formed behind Kohl's ears, "she was small enough to fit into my hand when I brought her home," looking dreamily at her palm.

"Remember the horses?" I said, wanting to prolong the pleasant mood. Nothing more was needed for each of us to nod and chuckle. A year before, David, Luce, and I had gone to the seashore with the dog. I untied her leash because we were alone on the beach, but a group of horses appeared and she went berserk, herding them ever tighter with barked enthusiasm until they all fit in a tight spot. The horses bumped rumps and heads trying to keep track of the dog while the riders, who had paid good money for a horseback stroll on the beach, yelled at me, "Control your dog!"

"You're supposed to keep it on a leash," one rider shouted, pointing at a sign I had seen and decided to ignore.

I shouted apologies at them and orders to the dog while we ran, also in circles, until David finally tackled her. The horses fled and we all fell into a heap together—dog, kids and I—panting and laughing.

I have often wondered with puzzled sorrow just how harmed my children were by the ethic of personal freedom and wide-open choices that I adopted, preferring the risks of exploration over the risks of suffocation. Such values were highly praised in the town where we raised them, to a degree that I found at times excessive and dangerous. Granted, I was not responsible for the drugs in middle school, grunge rock music, and the lyrics of Metallica or Jim Morrison, but I brought them to this place when they were way too young to face the boundless spaces of drugs and wilderness.

LOOKING FOR EDEN

I discovered the Northwest during a family camping trip in August 1980. I fell in love with it from the moment the Cascade Mountains revealed themselves after the long, hot expanse of Nebraska, Wyoming, and Idaho. The air was cool the next morning as I emerged from the tent next to a lively, chilly stream. The muted light filtering through the high canopy of impeccably straight Ponderosa pines, as in a cathedral, stirred up my reverence. This is sure to be the closest thing to Eden, I thought.

Beyond the pass, the moss and fallen logs in the forest smelled of ferment, growth, and decay, like the woods of my village. I could name every flower in the yards of the small towns where we stopped to eat, and my mother had grown the kind of vegetables and berries we bought at farm stands in the valley. Finally, the Pacific Ocean offered the bracing wind I knew from my grandmother's home on the North Sea, and I ate raw mussels straight from the rock, mouth and heart filled with the iodine taste of my childhood summers. Nature seemed to offer not only solace, but also the promise that I could be at home there in a complete, physical way that I had not felt in the past twelve years in the continental Midwest. The attraction was elemental, unreasoned. I spoke of moving during the whole trip back.

James, estranged from his mother and brothers since he'd

stopped drinking, agreed and began dreaming of attending architecture school. When I gave two months notice at the hospital where I worked and we put our house on the market, James and I both ignored what could go wrong. I'd find myself in private practice, without institutional backing, friends, or mentors. James would be separated from his sponsor and support groups, and from a town he'd known forever. And we'd all miss James' father, now sober for twelve years, and his second wife, who were wonderful grandparents.

Luce and David, six and three years old, would go along with any program, but Anna, ten and dramatic in her protest, dressed all in black to display her grief at leaving the friends she'd seen every day since preschool.

I am puzzled to contemplate a basic contradiction in me. Most of the time, I act on the belief that intelligent planning and diligence will ensure safe passage through the world and, I hope, contain its unpredictability as well as the wildness within me. But then I let it loose, throwing myself into a new adventure all of a sudden. I had done it again.

I've wondered since, if we were also moved by the unrecognized wish to distance ourselves from the recent painful memories that suffused our Kansas home. One afternoon in the previous summer, James had wanted to teach Luce, then four and a half, how to cross the street safely. "You've got to look both ways and make sure there is no car coming," he told her. "Now, tell me if you see one."

Standing on the curb, she swiveled her head several times, then said, "I see something there," pointing to her left. "I think it's big. It could be a car, but I can't tell if it's moving."

It was the middle of the day under a bright sky, and James couldn't believe his ears. Luce was nearly blind, yet this was the first indication she'd given either of us. Her vision had decreased gradually and she had thought nothing of it, too young to know what was normal or not.

She was diagnosed with congenital cataracts, complications from a viral infection contracted in utero that, for unknown reasons, develop around that age. Having had early years of normal vision, she'd learned the spatial skills that allowed her to function when her vision diminished. She knew her house by heart and was not yet learning to read, so we hadn't noticed her failing.

James and I were further shaken by erroneous information given to us by a nurse, indicating that Luce would never see much better. Soon came the operations and the sight of our tiny girl, puffy white bandages taped over her eyes, feeling her way through the house by following the top of the corridor's wainscoting with the tips of her fingers. I remember taking a hotel room one night after work so I could cry to my heart's content, away from the kids. I couldn't possibly whine when Luce did not even whimper. James took care of her with devotion. In the hospital, where they didn't yet have recliners for family, he spent nights sleeping on the floor beside her bed.

Time had seemed to drag until our 1980 summer trip. In contrast, after our decision to move, I felt the thrill of promise, the wide-open opportunity to start a new life in an edenic place. But we had entered a wilderness, stretched wide and unsecured. No moorings or tethers to tie us to safety, no one to recognize a cry of distress, no known voice to reassure and show the way.

Plenty did go wrong. Work was hard to come by. I opened my office just at the beginning of a steep economic decline that would last much of the eighties and, according to old timers, in our region would rival the Great Depression. Too few patients came to my office, reminding me of the bad times as a general practitioner in France, and our savings soon melted. James' special education credentials were not recognized in our new state, and he'd need two years to get a new certificate. Financial insecurity weighed heavily on us; James decided to stay home with the kids instead of going to architecture school, and I looked for every possible way to earn more money—evaluations at the hospital or jail, and consultations at alcoholism treatment centers.

More than the fatigue from work, I hated the long hours away from my children. Driving home through the last dregs of day-light, I physically felt the pull of longing as if it were a rope tied around my heart, and cried when the darkness of night meant the little ones would already be asleep.

I missed the children, and James was lonely. In January 1982, visiting his mother on her birthday, James took his first drink, the first alcohol he'd ingested since December 1974. He told me about it one evening a few months later. "I've been drinking since the beginning of the year." I stared, speechless, as he composed a non-chalant face. "It's not a problem—you didn't even notice." I stammered a few strangled sounds and he continued. "Got it under control. Not a problem," with a short slashing motion of his right hand. End of subject.

I gathered all possible cool thinking. "I am convinced it is a problem," I articulated painfully after a while, not wanting to meet his eye. "You have a serious disease and I believe that you are in relapse." I raised my hand to stop him when he cleared his throat, as if preparing for debate. "Let me finish. I've known for a long time that relapses are frequent in alcoholism and that it could happen to you. I just hope you get back to your program soon."

I congratulated myself for keeping my composure and went to bed right away while James stayed up. I even fell asleep. But at two in the morning I was in the bathroom, vomiting my guts out. I knew I was helpless to make him do anything he didn't choose. I could only hope that, after all he had learned during the previous seven years of sobriety, he would soon come back to his senses.

I went back to support groups to keep my fear, grief, and anger in check. I couldn't bring myself to leave him right away even though I had promised myself, in years past, never to live with a drinker again. But I thought of plenty of reasons for staying put just then. I loved him, yes, and was encouraged by the good years we'd had together and all that we shared—our children, first and foremost. He had an easy way with Luce and David and, even if Anna was more diffident because she remembered his fierce temper before sobriety, I reasoned that she'd be better off knowing her father well, warts and all, than not at all. Besides, in order to continue to work to raise them, I needed him to take care of the little ones.

And I especially needed him when Luce's congenital cataracts invaded her eyes again and needed to be removed. She was an old pro. She'd had surgeries on average once a year since her second birthday, knew the ropes, looked at the needle with interest instead of wriggling away when a nurse poked her arm to get a blood sample, and hospital staff called her "a good little trooper." Her ophthalmologist was particularly sweet to Luce and let me stay with her as long as possible on surgery day. I remember her tiny body covered with a sheet, lying on a gurney parked by the wall of a coldly lit corridor. Her eyes fastened on mine as I bent over her with words of love. Her hospital gown smelled of strong detergent and the neon light drained color from her cheeks. I held her hand and forgot all about the people in scrubs who glided on their paper overshoes behind me until one tapped my shoulder and said, "We've got to go now." Luce let herself be strapped to the gurney and smiled back at the anesthesiologist who engaged her in small talk. To this day my body can feel the sensation of her small hand slipping through my fingers and hear the swoosh of the operating room doors closing, catching a glance of the anesthesiologist before he pulled up his mask, snapped on his latex gloves, and injected her into oblivion.

James' dark moods returned with his drinking. Late in the evening, I forced myself to listen in silence to his monologues as he drank scotch and water by the window, staring into the darkness beyond. The complaints were familiar: no one appreciated or respected him. I reasoned that by draining some of the fetid emotions that inflamed him, I would protect our children, that their dad wouldn't show them during the day the bile he exuded as he drank well into the night. I was wrong. In spite of his devotion to the kids, he was antsy and reactive. He never hit any of us, but one could not predict when angry words would sting like lashes. Fear was ever present.

I lost my precarious balance when, in August 1982, I learned that one of my cousins had blown her brains out. She came from the part of my father's family where I can trace the strain of manic-depressive illness through the generations, expressed in variations from creative originality to mute despair. This cousin and I had been very close, so I felt awful that she hadn't called me to share her suffering. Receiving the news of her death, I sensed again in myself the strength of the suicidal impulse that had led her to the gun. As if she and I had been flying in the same contained aircraft, and the blast of the gun had torn the plane wall and I was getting sucked through the hole into a great void.

During the following months, I often felt ineffectual as bread-winner and worthless as a wife, expecting disaster, and the pain of living was so absolute at times that I could not conceive it would ever end. As if the certainty of failure had always been there and would always be there. Depression erased yesterdays and tomor-rows, the memory of having felt happy and strong in the past, as well as the hope I would be happy again. I was afraid I couldn't endure and would want out.

What I knew about my illness told me differently, but reason couldn't touch the feeling, and I dreaded that I might die at my own hand in spite of a clear intent to stay alive. So I used my con-scious mind to strap me to safety. I admonished myself: "Be care-ful, watch everything, and double check. You will want to ignore a signal, the sight of a car coming. It would look like an accident but it wouldn't be." I remember the specific sadness of not being able to trust my own self; I had lost my closest ally.

Fortunately I was able to fashion a survival kit made of what had helped me during previous encounters with depression: a psy-chiatrist who knew me well, medications that would eventually help, and friends to confide in.

Irascible father, preoccupied mother, sick little sister—these things were hard to take for Anna, then twelve. She too looked somber and unhappy, but refused to talk to me. For months I knocked on her bedroom door every night when I returned from work, and was told to go away. James and I insisted that she come to the table for dinner with all of us, where she ate in defiant silence.

We sought consultation from a child psychiatrist when Anna became more upset and tearful. "There is nothing wrong with this child," the doctor told us at the end of her examination. She pointed a finger at James. "You've got to stop drinking," then pointed at me, "and you stop crying. Then she'll be okay." Still, it took a long time to reach Anna again.

Gradually, my depression began to fade. Hope dawned and I could begin to use what I knew about living with an alcoholic: that, by changing what I could and accepting the rest, I could craft a good life. It had taken months of therapy, recovery meetings, and reflection, but one day I sensed I was back, that I'd regained the self I recognized as me. The healing was as mysterious as the illness, but finally the vigor of life reasserted itself in me.

I rented a two-room apartment, close to the grade school where Luce and David went, to take the children away from the sight of their father, now out-of-control drunk most nights. At night we stayed very close to each other and talked quietly until the children fell asleep, then I lay down in the bedroom we shared, happy from the sound of their breathing and little dreamy noises. In the morning before school, sitting cross-legged on the carpet, they ate the kind of single-boxed sugary cereals usually strictly reserved for camping, a tiny pleasure I could offer.

James stopped drinking in May 1983. I went back home two months later, wanting to rebuild the structure of the good years of recovery and keep our family intact. Every single one of us had been traumatized in the two and a half years since I had dreamt that we'd stumbled upon Eden. I thought the best way to heal was to give each other warmth, to huddle close, in order to withstand the real world's harshness.

I've asked myself in the years since why I returned home, really. I didn't have to. Many single moms raise three kids alone. So what if we'd lost all the equity put into the house because real estate

value had dropped during the recession? I had faced money problems before and survived. What is the nature of marital love and
attachment to someone you're temporarily mad at and yet committed to?

Equally mysterious, and possibly closer to the truth: I have a
strong affiliative need that I think is hardwired in most humans
and other mammals, expressed in loyalty to their tribe or pride.
As if the family was the basic organism whose survival may be
more essential than any individual's, the whole being greater than
the sum of the parts.

ROLLER COASTER

During the winter of 1991, after Luce returned from her long hospital stay, all of us drove once a week to a town an hour away for family therapy. The hospital psychiatrist had recommended the social worker we went to see, who had a long Indian name.

The first time, we left home well ahead of our appointment to take a quiet road that followed a river, passing tidy Mennonite farms with little girls in long flowered skirts playing on swings in front yards. James spoke little while driving on the windy road, and David and Luce were usually silent in the back. I let the tension from work seep out of me. The trees changing colors and the days shortening drastically from one week to the next put me in a meditative mood. What would the future bring?

The social worker's office was in his home. A gravel driveway wound through large rhododendron bushes that hid the weathered house. A short old man opened the door, said his name, and nodded as we introduced ourselves, shaking each of our hands in turn with soft words of welcome. His small hand was dry as silk, with a fleshy palm, his head dark and polished like driftwood, and the house smelled of cedar. He ushered us to a small, dark room with simple wooden chairs, a pale lampshade, brightly colored cushions decorated with tiny mirrors, and a statue of the Hindi goddess of compassion on a bookshelf.

He started by stating what he'd been told about Luce's problems and hospital stay, then gently asked questions. I could now only guess at the words he, and we in return, used, but I clearly remember that his soft voice had a quiet strength and that in his dark eyes shone an intelligence I immediately trusted. How I craved such qualities, how I needed such a person to steady our family circle at a time when it was wobbling like a warped wheel.

During the following sessions, each of us hesitated equally to speak first, so he made the rounds, asking about the previous week. I don't recall amazing revelations or breakthrough insights having been spoken in his room, but the roundness of his quiet body and careful speech infused calm in the dim space, and I wanted to believe in his wisdom.

So I told him my confusion about the recent years of our family life, when Luce was fourteen to sixteen, where much good had seemed to take place while she secretly fell apart. Since James had stopped drinking, eight years before, honest communication between us had cleared the way for renewed closeness. We'd attended recovery meetings and personal growth seminars. We trusted words and explanations. James had gathered a solid social group around him. He meticulously prepared the bicycling tours through France that he led in the summers. At home, he was at his best when we invited friends over, proud to show off the flowers he tended in the garden and to surprise guests with unusual combinations of spices at dinner. We enjoyed discussing movies or politics, attending concerts and being loudly competitive at Scrabble. We talked a lot, about important and trivial things, and I relied on him, who read the newspaper front to back every morning, to keep me abreast of local news. With a now successful professional life, I felt secure and rarely cried anymore. Until, that is, Luce had almost killed herself.

I am reminded of a quote by H.L. Mencken, the journalist who covered the Scope's trial: "Penetrating so many secrets, we cease to believe in the unknowable. But there it sits nevertheless, calmly licking its chops."

If our life were so wonderful, why did our daughter want to

die? That reality shut me up. So I turned to our host, the expert in family dramas with the goddess of compassion on his shelf. He drew each of us in by simple questions.

I may not recall his words but I remember the lilt and foreign cadences of his phrases as he encouraged one of us, then the other, to speak of our fears, of death, anger, and despair. I can still hear Luce's voice, husky from barely contained tears: "I don't know why. I just know I want to die. It's so strong. I'm tired of fighting it." I hear James: "I'm so scared. And I don't know what to do," his voice cracking into a child-like tone. And David: "I don't want anything bad to happen." I feel the hot tears that tightened my cheeks, the breath that caught in my throat.

But later in the session, as the darkness of the winter evening shut out the world beyond the windows, making the warm little room feel insular, I watched James' shoulders lose their tension, Luce's eyes shine brighter, and David flash a smile as the therapist kept coming back to the palpable love manifested by the simple fact that we were all together, in this room, without shields or weapons. My heart lightened and peace followed me home.

Luce continued to be slowed down by sadness for several months, with little hope and even less desire for a future she couldn't imagine. She was often in bed when called for dinner and looked at food on her plate as if it were a smelly dead fish. Wrinkled shirts hung loose over her bones. She didn't call friends on the phone and I had forgotten the sound of her laugh. She did not respond well to medication, needing higher doses than most people for a therapeutic effect that was never as complete as could be hoped for, and she suffered side effects. In that way also she resembled her father, whose recurrent depressions were hard to treat.

Yet, little by little, she got better.

I regretted that, when she went back to the university in January 1992, we had to stop family meetings with the Indian gentleman because of scheduling conflicts.

Luce took a few classes at first, more the next term, and did a full term of chemistry in six weeks during summer session. We bought her a used Geo Metro, a bright-blue tin box on wheels, and she took her dog, head out of the passenger door window and long tongue lolling in the wind, to hot springs in the mountains or the windy beaches of the Pacific. Her appetite returned, for tasty food, jazz and dance, friends and laughter, and by summer, glossy long hair and tawny skin, she was beautiful again.

James and I felt safe leaving her home by herself to complete her classes when we took David to Anna's graduation from New York University in May 1992. We squeezed into a crowd gathered on Washington Square to cheer the graduates under a sunny sky. The students' shiny gowns fluttered, and high, excited voices covered the commencement speech. I barely caught a glimpse of Anna on the stage. But I was happy to be back for a week in the thrill of Manhattan. I showed David a favorite display of mine at the Metropolitan Museum: the ancient miniature clay figurines depicting daily life in pharaonic Egypt, similar to those I had sought at his age every time I went to the Louvre. James and I got our fill of foreign movies and new plays. I drank up the energy of crowds on the sidewalks, thirsty for the high rhythms of accents from the boroughs and the intensity of conversations in the Village coffee shop next to our hotel.

Anna stayed on in New York to start her theater career and invited Luce and Josh to visit during summer vacation. They stayed a week together in August, the girls intent on becoming good friends as grown-up sisters.

November 7, 1992. A year after Luce's near-death, the hospital, and the long sad winter. I flung a white embroidered tablecloth over the dining room table and David helped me set plates, crystal water glasses, and the silverware we'd been given as a wedding present. He lit candles. I forget what James cooked, but it had to be something Luce particularly liked, maybe shrimp stir-fry and chocolate cake. We were celebrating her eighteenth birthday.

She came in with Josh and flashed, with a flourish, the ring he'd just given her. At once proud and shy, Josh explained he had designed it himself, and Luce pulled it off her finger so we could each admire the curving lines and the luster of the gold.

After the cake, the blown candles, and the song, Luce grinned, flipped her hair and said, "This *is* a happy birthday. I never thought it could happen."

When school started in September, she had moved to a one-room apartment a few blocks from the university. A photo shows her proprietary smile when she opened the door on her first day there, long bare arms gleaming in the sun. She looks like any young woman at the beginning of her adult life, welcoming the challenge. Impressed by her resilience, I allowed myself to be as hopeful as she seemed.

I recently found a short audiotape made by Luce around that time. She recorded an interview she'd requested with a psychologist, an old friend from our Kansas years. He happened to be the supervisor of the psychologist who'd administered testing to Luce during her hospitalization the previous year; she wanted to ask him to explain the test results.

I was struck by Luce's tone of voice when I listened to the tape, how stable, reflective and well-organized she sounded. Independent from the fact that I also delighted in hearing again her contralto sound, a little hushed yet lustrous.

At the beginning, she sounded matter-of-fact and clinical, as if she were a student and the psychologist her teacher, commenting on someone else. She read sentences from the report that she wished to clarify, responding mostly with "Hu-hums" to his detailed explanations. But a more animated exchange followed her questions about instances when she'd shown impaired thinking. "Are these findings permanent, or do they change?" she asked, and later, "Where does the distorted thinking come from?"

The psychologist mentioned links between heat of emotion and thought impairment, but also alluded to long-standing patterns of thought based on a highly personal view of the world. The following is a near-verbatim transcription:

"My guess is it goes back to your growing up years. You said in some tests that others can be hurtful rather than helpful. That would lead to isolation, where you keep to your own counsel, stay out in a corner where you can figure out everything on your own. There is some danger to that."

She laughed heartily. "You can figure out anything you want."

He chuckled too. "But it leaves you unmoored. That's the price."

"It's a huge price . . . That makes sense to me, the mental isolation."

A few moments later, she reflected, "I'm surprised by the comment on my self-image as injured and attacked." But when I heard this, I wasn't surprised. Sharp images flooded my mind, of Luce as a little girl being wheeled time and again into operating rooms to be anesthetized and cut open, subjected to physical pain and incomprehensible loss of consciousness at the hands of doctors claiming to wish her well, with her parents standing by and letting it all happen. What could she have figured out in her two-year-old mind the first time it happened, or even at eight when she'd had the last eye surgery?

At eighteen, in the psychologist's office, she wanted to understand. She went on, reading from the report. "I'm curious about 'interesting contrast between weak and passive and actively playing dangerous games.'"

"When one feels victimized," explained the psychologist, "that the world is not a trustable good place, several responses are possible. One, the most common, is to roll over. You do a little of that. The second is to be suspicious, fight back. Not much of that in your stories. You produced an intriguing third possibility. As if you could play at the edge of danger. Of the order of someone who has a clear sense of firearms as dangerous and doesn't particularly want to die, but gets a kick out of playing Russian roulette anyway. You choose to be out there, active—"

Luce interrupted. "Challenge," she said quietly.

"—not only not rolling over, but pushing yourself where it's more dangerous, jumping in instead of running away. Kind of 'I'll show you.'"

"Yeah," said Luce with a big laugh. Then, in an animated voice:

"I'll jump out of the pan into the fire—*on purpose*," those last words spoken with great emphasis.

The psychologist laughed with her. "Which leaves everybody else in your life going oh— oh—."

Luce added, with a quieter laugh, "Yeah. I've certainly done my share of that." Then, after a long silence, "Okay."

The therapist concluded the interview with, "The cure is to find a few people you trust enough to check yourself with. It's good to do your own careful checking in your therapy."

"Yeah," Luce answered thoughtfully. Do I read too much into her tone, which to me sounds somewhat dubious?

A roller-coaster ride was not only Luce's fate, but that of Anna as well. Early in 1993 in New York, Anna walked home at night with a girlfriend. They were crossing the street when a car, rounding the corner too fast, slid on an icy patch and barreled into her. Her head hit the windshield with enough force to break the thick glass, and she was thrown to the frozen ground.

The driver stopped only long enough to check if Anna was alive and tell her friend that he had no insurance. Then he drove away. Anna's friend was too shaken to insist that he give his name. Anna was dazed and told me later that, had she been alone, she's certain she would have lain in the frozen gutter and died of the cold. "We were on First Street by the Bowery, where people are used to stepping over drunks and junkies. No one there would've stopped for me, until maybe the next morning when it was too late."

Anna's friend took her to the emergency room in a cab. Anna hated the long wait and only wanted to be back home and go to sleep. A rapid exam by an overworked ER doctor showed large bruises where her back had slammed onto the pavement, but no broken bones on X-rays. She appeared coherent, could state the correct date and name the president, so she was released from the hospital without a follow-up appointment.

James and I flew to New York right away. Anna was convinced that she'd be better in no time and only needed some rest in a quiet place far from the city. We took her to a hotel on the closest

sunny Caribbean island. It faced a calm lagoon-like bay, the color
of turquoise, edged by a thin crescent of sand, with a background
of palm fronds. The shallow water, warm and clear, seemed perfect for a girl who'd been a competitive swimmer and found solace
in the water. Yet not only could Anna not swim, she could not
even float on her back because the minute movements needed to
keep her balance sent spasms all along her spine. On those days,
her highest achievements were leafing through magazines on the
beach and watching a little television.

She insisted on returning to her New York apartment after a
few days, and didn't want us to take her to a doctor. Afraid we'd
insist she fly back with us, she didn't tell us that her whole back
was knotted in pain and her thinking loopy from the severe con-
cussion. She wanted to return to work as soon as possible, and get
on with her promising life as a performer.

It took her several more weeks to fully realize that, still unable
to carry a half-full bag of groceries up to the second floor where
she lived alone, and unable to think clearly enough to go to work,
she could not care for herself. She finally moved back home, to
rest and start physical therapy.

Living in our house was something she had thought never to do
again after leaving for college, and she dreaded it. She had clashed
with both her father and me in her teens but, at this point, each
of us was determined to start afresh. I was bending over the dish-
washer one evening and caught a glimpse of Anna sitting at the
dinner table, dirty plate and glass in front of her. The words "Anna,
can't you get up and clear your own plate?" almost spilled from my
lips, but I checked myself in time. I remembered the exaspera-
tion that such a phrase would have carried ten years before. She
would've answered, "You always make me do more than the others," and we'd have been bickering, throwing *always* and *never* until
she retreated in anger and I in frustration. How incredibly trivial
that now seemed. It was easy not to nag any longer.

Until one late evening after an exhausting day at work when I
saw, next to her on the living room couch from where she watched
TV, a mound of her unfolded clothes that I had gotten out of the

dryer that morning. This time I spoke before I could stop myself. "Anna, quit that stupid program and fold your clothes. You've had all day—"

"Mom," she said, raising calm eyes to meet mine. "Stop." Her gaze was wonderfully strong. I sat beside her and apologized. "Wow," she laughed, "I never thought I'd have the guts to say that to you. And you did it!" she added with peals of laughter, "you just stopped." By then I was laughing too.

Within three months, it became clear that Anna's healing would be slow. The true impact of a closed head injury like the one she had suffered reveals itself gradually; loss of memory and moments of confusion plagued her. And she had to work tirelessly with a physical therapist to deal with the chronic inflammation caused by the massive back trauma.

With grief in her heart, she broke the lease on her New York apartment and rented a studio a couple of miles from our home, close to high school friends. She started working with her beloved high school drama teacher and performed in local theaters, finding that memorizing roles was the best therapy for her brain damage. Recovery would take years, but she did it. In the meantime, she also grew close to the young man she would later marry, a tall red-haired sweetheart of a guy finishing a fine arts degree.

The trip we took in 1993, before Luce's summer school session, was the first one for the whole family in many years, since Anna had stopped coming along at sixteen. After my mother's death in 1986, the pull to spend family vacations every other year in France diminished. James and I had fallen in love with Indonesia when we'd gone to Bali with friends, and wanted to return. Luce decided she had to see the Komodo dragons, the carnivorous giant lizards that live only on a remote Indonesian island.

First we stayed on a minuscule coral islet in thatched huts without electricity, spending hours swimming with darting fish of all colors. I remember the giggles punctuating the conversations of the three kids in the hut next door before sleep. Anna was four and a half years older than Luce, seven and a half older than

David. They were little kids when she'd left for New York. But now they had caught up with her, David towering over his sisters at fifteen, and the three talked and hung out together by choice, not parental demand.

The simplicity of the place made us naturally gather up close, like large primates grooming each other. We brought fruit or chicken skewers with peanut sauce to our huts and lathered lotion on each other's backs. James and I, our bodies blessed by sun, water, and beauty, found each other in the pleasure of being lovers and parents.

Anna's back still hurt, so she stayed in a country hotel in Bali while the rest of us went along the archipelago, using crowded local buses full of curry smells and steaming-hot metal ferries reeking of rust. The slow rhythms of such travels lulled me into quiet contemplation, and the deliberate happiness and smiling courtesy of Indonesians was contagious. I had learned no more than a few dozen words of Bahasa Indonesia, just enough to exchange some pleasantries and trigger gales of laughter in women at the markets. I loved how close they came, holding my hand and looking straight at me with loving eyes, caressing Luce's cheek while cooing in appreciation of her youth and beauty. David was at first dismayed when young men held his hand in friendship while talking to him, but soon got accustomed to the gentle gestures of welcome.

The dragons of Komodo Island looked the part, ten feet long with powerful stubby legs and claws, dragging a massive tail in the sand. They had the run of the national park that covered the whole island. They moved impossibly fast for their two hundred pounds. We were told that the adult dragons ate their own young if they could, so the smaller ones sought the relative protection of the few huts set up for guides and tourists. At night, we could hear their thrashing beneath the thatched hut on stilts were we stayed, accompanied by the squeals and grunts of wild boars that reminded me of childhood hunts with my father in our village.

Luce had listened, enraptured, to an information lecture given by a park employee and couldn't wait for the hike into the forest the next day. Stories of dark wildness arrested her, fitting with her bleak view of the laws of nature as favoring predators. Guides led us in the early morning to an enclosed viewpoint space at the top of a cliff, overlooking a sandy clearing. We could hear dragons move through the bushes below. A young man explained that they would come to the clearing to be fed. The meal would be the goat which he had led on a leash during the walk, and his colleague would now prepare the food. We should stay where we were.

Another young man dragged the bleating goat behind a bamboo blind. Luce followed him quietly and looked on as he deftly cut the goat's throat, then went to the edge of the cliff and threw the carcass down. It had barely settled on the ground when dragons ran from different directions and tore into its gleaming red flesh, fighting for it with fierce swings of the jaws and neck, and swipes of their mighty front paws.

Most tourists, including David, James, and me, squirmed and alternated between bending forward to look and averting our eyes, making little moans. But Luce stood transfixed, immobile at the edge of the cliff, absorbing sights and sounds, her face a mask of concentration. She did not speak on the hike back, but asked for paper as soon as we returned to the park's meeting room. She wrote furiously on the rickety bare wood table of our hut that afternoon, three tightly packed pages I found later with her private journals. She wrote from the point of view of the goat, describing in details the experience of losing life.

I'd noticed her intensity on that day, and asked, "What were you thinking about this morning?"

"It was interesting," she said in a casual tone, with a dismissive shrug, "nothing more," folding the pages and putting them away. But she confided much later that the experience had stayed with her. She could totally identify with the slain animal, she told me with some wonder, feel its physical pain, but no fear at all. Death was its fate, as it should be. I shuddered, reminded she'd used the same words about herself two years before, after trying to hang herself.

Luce took premed science classes that summer and looked strong, healthy, and ambitious. Yet there were reminders of her fragility. In early summer, she had called, speaking in a very young and frightened voice. "Mom, my tummy hurts very bad." When I arrived at her apartment, she was doubled-up in pain and, suspecting appendicitis, I took her to the emergency room. I held one of her hands while we waited, and she pressed her other hand on her belly. Still, she tried to smile and even made a joke or two.

How many hours had we spent together in waiting rooms? Hundreds. We were used to this, barely scared, holding hands and talking. Each time in the past, especially before her surgeries, I had tried to explain what went on inside her body and what she could expect from the procedures. She said that it helped her to know as much as possible beforehand. It helped me too to feel useful.

She looked at the other people in the ER waiting room and made up stories about them. "Look at that guy with the mullet haircut, he's so strung out," she whispered. I joined her game. "Probably straight from a meth lab or something," I added. We chuckled, guilty for being mean.

It felt like business as usual when we were shown into an exam room. Luce lay on a table while a nurse checked her vital signs, then we were left to wait for a doctor. Suddenly, Luce got up and started pacing the small room rapidly, back and forth, wrapping the light hospital gown around her, arms and hands tight around her waist. Her face had drained of color and she breathed hard. She moaned and mumbled, "The smell, the smell."

I tried to touch her but she pushed my hand aside and continued to walk fast, trembling, a haunted look in her eyes that darted here and there.

"What's going on?"

"I don't know, Mom. I'm afraid." She looked around, chin up, alert, as if checking for danger, then shook her head. "I don't know."

I faced her and placed my hands lightly on each of her arms, murmuring, "You're okay, okay," my words slow, separated by deep breaths. "You'll be all right."

Her wide eyes, fixed on mine, steadied. When she let me hold her close, I felt her heart beating fast through her slender chest, her rapid breaths into my ear, the sweat slicking her forehead against my cheek. Then the tension left her and she sat on a stool, exhausted, leaning against me.

"It's that smell," she said, pointing to the alcohol-filled containers, like narrow vases, where metal surgical instruments were stored. "Like when I was little, before an operation." She seemed absent, as if speaking from far away, from that other time.

I was sure I knew what was going on; I had seen it many times. "That was a flashback," I explained. "Smell is powerful that way, it brings back vivid memories." That caught her attention. She looked my way and I felt she was back with me. "You had an anxiety attack."

She looked puzzled, disturbed. "But I was never afraid of hospitals, I'm so used to them. I've been going there forever."

"You had to be afraid. Anybody is afraid when they go through surgery. I'm sure your body was scared, but you ignored it." I remembered well my own upbeat encouragements, how tightly I had held in my tears and worry. "You were very tough, and we all encouraged you. Dad and your doctors, and me too."

"I didn't feel scared then." She stopped talking for a while, looking all around the small hospital exam room, then bent her head. "But today, it was terrible." She was breathing fast again, eyes filling with tears.

"You know too much now. You're older. It's harder to put things out of your mind." I cried with her then, flooded with memory. "It was awful, all those operations when you were little."

"It was hard, Mom, it really was."

"I'm so sorry, my love." I rocked her.

She was still a courageous warrior. Three days after an appendectomy she was back in school.

She worked hard that summer and learned a lot. My heart swelled with pleasure when we met at small cafes by the university for lunch and she beamed with the excitement of discovery. I remembered my own wonder as a student of biology and physiology, my delight in the beauty and rightness of structures seen through a microscope, in the brilliance of colors in the chemistry lab. I still kept small stoppered vials filled with pure copper, cobalt and manganese powders on my window sill where light played with their vibrant colors. Luce's similar love for the thrill of science was a precious gift, reminding me how much I had loved and learned from my profession.

UNRAVELING

I n September 1993, at the start of her third year at the university, Luce enrolled in premed classes, and I hoped that over time she would receive as many gifts from medicine as I had. She and Josh planned to move together to a house with a couple of friends. Luce was excited to try on this next step to adulthood. I knew little of her daily life with Josh, who was restrained whenever we met and rarely came to our house, but I was grateful for his steadiness throughout the previous two years. In October we helped Luce move into a studio above the garage of the house where her friends lived in a residential neighborhood away from student apartment complexes. There was much anticipation of the fun they'd have together, as soon as Josh joined her.

But every week he had another excuse for not moving in, and Luce believed less and less in the reasons he gave for his delays. He still had not packed when she showed up at his house one evening, and they had it out. No, he was not coming, he told her. He didn't want that kind of commitment. As a matter of fact, he had not wanted it for some time. As a matter of fact, if she really wanted to know, he was going out with another girl. That's right, her friend. How long? A few months now. Luce screamed at him before slamming the door.

She told me all this only much later. She was ashamed of having been blind to Josh's unfaithfulness and didn't want her friends to know, so she stayed away even from her housemates. Anna would have listened to her, but Luce kept her distance from her as well, not returning calls.

Not wanting us to know of the breakup either, she rarely came home, pretending that classes kept her busy. When she later off-handedly mentioned that she and Josh were not together any-more, I asked, "Why don't you move back with us, you must be really lonely."

"No, no," she quickly answered, "everything's going to be all right."

I can't figure out why Luce was in our bedroom early one Sunday morning. She usually slept late and we got up early. But I remem-ber being in bed with the newspaper, ensconced in pillows with a coffee cup in hand, when she announced that she had started drinking again.

"Some," she said. "I have decided that I can drink some now, moderately." She sounded controlled and reasonable. "A glass of wine with dinner, or a beer."

I was speechless. I had been comforted that she hadn't used alcohol or drugs since her treatment long ago, as I knew they'd aggravate her depression. My apprehension rose, but she seemed to have none.

My memory of that Sunday is sharp. I see her walking back and forth in the pale morning light, cocky, straight-shouldered. Her legs were long in tight jeans, thighs round and strong.

"But . . ." James sat up straight and leaned forward, his hand on the comforter next to my knee.

"I know, I've been to enough meetings about sobriety." She raised a hand to prevent protest and her silver rings glittered. "I said I'm an alcoholic and an addict. But I was thirteen when I got in trouble, and I'm different now. I've been clean and sober all those years. Now I can handle it."

She put a lot of conviction in her voice, fastening her royal blue gaze on us.

Fear sat at my core, a palpable weight like granite. I remembered

James using similar words early in his relapse and the damage that relapse had done to him, to all of us.

He got out of bed before I could talk. His voice rang out, urgent. "Not true. You start and you may never get sober again. It can kill you."

I stood up as well. "You shouldn't drink when you're on lithium. And alcohol makes depression worse."

She deflected our words of caution with a stop gesture of the hand and stood her ground. "Anyway, I'm over eighteen," ignoring the twenty-one-year drinking age. "I can do what I want. I only want to tell you so you know. I didn't want you to find out by accident." She left the room. Then I heard the sound of her car.

Now we know, I thought as she drove away. I guess I should be grateful for small favors.

"At least she's honest." James' words echoed my thoughts. "Let's watch and see." His face, blue eyes washed gray by fear, mirrored the anxious squeeze of my heart. We hugged in silence.

We were wrong to place hope in her being open with us, because she would not be honest. And Luce was wrong in stating that she could handle her situation. She went back to her studio, to her lonely grief, ashamed that she missed Josh, hiding how much she wanted to cry all the time. When she finally told me, weeks later, why he'd left her, she snickered, "I'm pathetic, just a girl who falls apart because a guy leaves her. It's disgusting!"

College courses were hard and, in addition, she found that she was unable to do the extensive reading required. Even though she added reading glasses to her contact lenses, within an hour her vision became wavy, unfocused, and migraine set in, so that she couldn't keep up with homework.

David, in contrast to Luce, reached the bloom of his adolescence. A rapid growth spurt put him at eye level with the taller boys in his class, and he joined friends who had their own cars to snowboard or camp. For his sixteenth birthday in early November, a group of his friends came to play on the trampoline, doing outrageous tricks like jumping with their snowboards on. I would've been horrified if I'd seen them, fearing an accident, but it had been a while since I'd felt a need to supervise David's games. Most of the time he showed good sense and good balance.

The bunch of boys who'd been challenging each other on the trampoline stormed into the house, jostling and teasing one another with dramatic gestures and loud voices. They crowded around the kitchen table for the requisite pizza and root beer, not even seeing, I'd bet, James and me, who served them with grins on our faces. David, with his gentle brown eyes, widow's peak over a broad forehead, square shoulders, and tender smile, looked like the best of my French uncles. His dad too was unfailingly proud of him.

David beamed when the guys belted "Happy Birthday." He'd barely blown out the candles on the cake when Luce walked in the room with a present. Silence fell upon the group. One of the boys, we knew, had a crush on her and was often tongue-tied in her presence, but the others stared wide-eyed, their mouths shut tight. It was clear that her gray complexion, sad hollow face, and slow motions scared them. David's happy expression shut off like a slammed door.

Once more, Luce's suffering darkened the celebration of David's birthday, four days ahead of hers. Once more, in the season of waning light and chilled bones that marked her birthday, she slid into despair.

Over the next weeks, James or I went regularly to check on her, encourage her, bring her food or take her out, but not too often because she'd decided that, at nineteen, she was a grownup and needed to be in charge of her life. It seemed to be a sad lonely life, so we asked her to move back home, but she would not. And as long as she was in school, we thought we'd keep our agreement to support her in living on her own.

James too had trouble with depression that fall and winter of 1993. Every five years or so, a deep wave flattened him for months. During the long years of sobriety, he did everything he was supposed to do: antidepressants, psychotherapy, recovery groups. Yet the depressive episodes were severe and left him every time more exhausted and jaded.

His desk was a mess and he cursed when he was unable to find a paper or his keys. I thought a new medication made him more disorganized, although he insisted he was only energized. "Look," I told him, "I don't think this treatment is right for you." I thought his psychiatrist needed to know what I saw. "Let me come with you to your next appointment."

"Quit managing me!" he shouted, wagging his index finger close to my nose. "I forbid you to talk to my doctor."

He seemed disgusted with every comment or suggestion I made and we argued more than usual. "Damn it," I thought, "I quit." I decided to keep my distance so I wouldn't get frustrated and fight with him. After all, I had plenty to occupy me, taking care of patients who actually wanted to hear my opinions, and worrying about two sick daughters who at least let me embrace them without kicking.

David was the only child left at home, and he too needed me. A junior in the International High School, bright and sturdy, he brought in mostly B grades, teasing me with a consistent C in French. Several teachers argued that he could be an A student if he did the homework they expected, and that we should make him do it. Fat chance, to make David do what he didn't want to do. Since preschool he had performed at the top for some teachers and gone on strike with others, driving them nuts with his cheerful stubbornness.

That didn't surprise me; I too am stubborn, a family trait. But some teachers insisted we lean on David. James, protective of his son, said to me, "You make sure he does his homework. I don't want to get mad at him."

One late afternoon I stood over David, seated at the kitchen table, as he leafed limply through school notes in search of homework assignments.

"Oh," I stomped my foot, "you're so passive-aggressive!"

He lifted an unruffled face, brown eyes amused. "You've taught me that, very well. You don't get mad but you only do what you want."

I burst out laughing. "You're too smart for your own good. And for mine."

There was laughter in my life. Like with David, or when I met friends for lunch and walks. I have been blessed with an innate ability for joy that bubbles easily in me except during the severe depressions I've had four times in my life. Even after months of low moods, I recovered completely and regained a buoyancy that reminds me of my grandmother, who soothed us with bedtime stories during the war. I remember how my kids would groan and roll their eyes when we were driving for a day's adventure and I'd burst out singing *my* song, off-key: "I am the child of Mother Nature and Father Time, fecund, full of eggs, and full of beans." I have worked hard to deal with traumas and temper my neurotic traits, but that inborn, undeserved talent for enjoying life is a gift I can only give thanks for and celebrate.

Luce had no such luck. Happiness didn't come easily to her beyond her early years, and especially not at that time. She looked sad and sick again. She didn't tell us of course, even though we asked, that she often got drunk. Not after trying to convince us that she could safely drink "some," or "moderately," as she'd said that Sunday morning in our bedroom. In addition, as recorded in another journal that she began to write around her nineteenth birthday, she started using hallucinogens—mushrooms and acid. To my knowledge, she did not confide in her friends. Only the strangers from whom she bought the stuff, as she wrote in the journal, or met in bars late at night when she couldn't sleep.

I called her almost every day, and it was clear from the low energy of her tone that she was having a hard time, but she wouldn't be specific and soon hung up. "I'm okay, don't worry," seemed a mantra. But when I asked about her studies, she said, in an unusually thin and whiny voice, "It's hard, Mom. I can't read all that homework. My head hurts so much I can't see straight. I can't stand the light of day." She quit attending classes before Thanksgiving, but kept that to herself as well so that we wouldn't make her come home. Once more, depression swallowed the outside world and she lived alone, in darkness.

I went a couple of times a week to visit her in the upstairs studio she'd moved into—could it have been only two months before? It seemed another life—in joyous anticipation of her life with Josh. The way to her room was a severely crooked stairway, which now was decorated with what looked to me like instruments of death and pain. In the corner of a landing stood a lance that she'd found I don't know where, probably when she and her first boyfriend had camped with the Society for Creative Anachronism, play-acting medieval jousting. A knife and gothic insignia, which reminded me of punk graffiti in the seedy alleys downtown, were mounted on the wall. A wounded doll hung by her neck from a nail.

"I hate this," I told her, "it gives me the creeps every time I walk up here. It can't be good for you to see this. Take it down."

"Oh, Mom. Don't make too much of it," she laughed. "Remember, I've had things like that in my room since I was thirteen."

"Yeah, and I've hated them since then."

"Well, I still love Anne Rice and I'm not dead yet."

Small comfort for me to hear those words as I stood in the large dark room under a sloping roof that forced her to bend or crawl to reach things stored against the walls. Drapes were always shut over the two large skylights that I knew could have revealed lovely views of the south hills, and the bed remained unmade. Candles and incense burned on the bedside table, and I recognized the Jim Morrison tapes that frightened me. The words, describing a long journey at the edges of destruction, and the wailing voice, gripped my heart with dread.

One late afternoon I came by to find Luce still in bed, her fine oval face deformed by a bulging bruise. She told me she'd fallen and hit her cheekbone on the edge of the coffee table. She said a migraine had felled her. I sat beside her, gently held her wounded face in my hands, and asked her again about drugs.

Scrupulous honesty had been the foundation of the recovery program she followed in her teenage years. But, now, she swore that she did not use. She looked at me straight, and I didn't know what to do but love her. I accepted depression as the cause for her disordered room and ravaged face. One more breakdown.

Luce lied and lied some more. In her journal she wrote obsessively of solitude, her wish for love, tenderness, and sex, and her despair at not finding them. She wrote about how hallucinogens took her out of that unbearable reality into a world of colors, a world that she didn't need to make sense of.

Mother and psychiatrist, I was torn between loving acceptance and a sense of responsibility for her condition. She was of age, so I couldn't force her to have drug tests against her will. In early December though, on another visit when I found her listless in bed at six p.m., surrounded by an utter chaos of clothes, empty glasses, and cigarette smoke, I pushed. "Luce, you can't go on like this. We've got to go together to talk to your doctor."

"Oh, all right," she answered in a lifeless voice, without raising her head.

The next day, Luce sat nearly mute in a deep chair across from the psychiatrist's desk, barely moving for almost an hour, wrapped in her long wool coat, hair hanging over sunken cheeks. I asked my colleague what she thought of Luce's response to the medications.

When I described how bad things had looked for weeks and the mess in her house, the doctor seemed surprised. "I saw her last week," she said, frowning and checking her notes. "No, make that two weeks ago, she cancelled last week's appointment. Well, last time, she told me she was okay, and she looked alright. Not happy, don't misunderstand me, but not like today."

"Luce is very good at making herself look much better than she is," I responded, "at least for a little while. But now she's really down, she hardly does anything. Should she be in the hospital?"

Luce looked up then. "Oh no, not there," she pleaded, shaking her head. As the doctor asked her specific questions about sleep, activity, mood, appetite, suicidal thoughts, she kept her eyes straight on the doctor's face, earnestly answering in a voice that seemed to convey the truth. That's when I learned she'd dropped out of school a month before and could hardly sleep because she felt so anxious, but was too bone-tired to get herself up. "I'm not hungry so I don't eat. But no, I don't want to kill myself. I just don't know what to do." Her voice cracked then and she started crying. Turning her devastated eyes toward me she repeated, shaking her head again and again, "Mom, I don't know what to do."

The psychiatrist spoke gently. "I don't think you need to be in the hospital just yet." Then, her voice sterner, "But you can't stay alone. You must go to your parents.'"

Luce put her head down and remained silent during the rest of the session, while her doctor gave me instructions on how to adjust the lithium and antidepressants.

Luce didn't use drugs at our home, but neither did she reconnect with her recovering friends or her sponsor. I imagine that her shame and self-loathing were too great to face the people who for many years had praised her for her sobriety. Her weight inched up week by week and she slept halfway well. "Not great but enough," as she put it, so that she could go for walks with the dog who ran circles around her, barking her joy at seeing Luce again and jumping up to lick her face. Those moments brought our lost daughter back for a short while, breaking through the mask of suffering that had hidden her for too long.

In January 1994, Luce began classes at a community college and in a few weeks got a licensed practical nurse certification. She wouldn't talk much about her courses or her teachers. "It's okay, Mom," she told me in a terse, matter-of-fact voice, bracing herself against the letdown from her dream. "I don't think I'll ever be a doctor. I can't hack it," she said with an aggressive thrust of her chin, as if defying herself to be sad.

"Anyway," she added, "I want to earn my own money. I want to be financially independent and live on my own." She got work as a home-health nurse and in late March moved to a dingy street-level studio close to downtown.

Her main pleasure was to ride the used Honda Elite scooter she asked me to buy, as David now drove the blue Geo Metro that used to be hers. James, sensibly enough, had objected to the scooter, but finally threw up his hands and went along after Luce passed the motorcycle safety class we'd required she take first. She learned to slalom through the orange cones on the practice course and to take ninety-degree corners sharply, proud of her mastery. I'm amazed that she could pass the vision test for the motorcycle driver's license; she told me later that she brazenly guessed at what she couldn't see for sure. I remember riding with her a few times through the hills on a country road, enjoying the unrestricted view of fields, mountains, and sky, and the fresh air like water on my skin, body leaning through the curves in a sort of dance. We were laughing from the same delight when we stopped and pulled off our helmets.

I realize now that by offering her the chance to ride, I wanted to make up for the emptiness of her life, for her sorrow over losing the future she'd dreamed of. After dropping out of school three years in a row, I too doubted she'd make it to medical school. I could still hear her as a child, "What I want is your life, to be a doctor and a mom," and felt I should've been able to make it possible for her.

James took Luce out to lunch regularly, where he said they discussed their experiences of depression and addiction, finding themselves alike in their outlook on life. She and I also met for a quick bite at noon on her days off. I often chose a small place across the street from my office. One day not long after she'd started a new job, Luce told me about her patient while I ate my sandwich in a hurry. "It's a long way to where she lives, I hate it when it rains." Her shoulders shook in a mock shiver as she warmed her hands on a coffee cup. I noticed with pleasure how much more expressive she'd become as her mood lifted. She wasn't above clowning when she recounted quirky encounters with the gallery of odd characters peopling downtown. In fact, I thought, she could pass for one of them, with a skull ring on her finger, a miniskirt over tattered leggings, and high heels, topped by a man's heavy leather jacket. A good thing she hadn't gotten into tattoos and piercings.

"But I like the lady," she continued, talking about the client she visited four days a week. "She's tiny, and so old she can't do much. But she's still pretty sharp. Not like that lady, remember, at the nursing home, during my training?" I must have made a face indicating I didn't know whom she meant. "The one I asked, 'You're Jane, right?' and she laughed and patted my hand." Luce mimicked the Alzheimer patient, "'Oh honey, how should I know?'"

I laughed in recognition. "Sure, I remember," and she joined me with a genuinely happy laugh, to my ears the sweetest sound in the world.

She selected which stories to tell. She said nothing then of going to drink in the evenings at a bar called Doc's Pad and stumbling back in the dark to her place. She was good at deflecting, charming, evading, conning when I tried to assess the extent of her drinking (and I didn't even suspect drug use right then). She looked straight at me with a loving shimmer in her eyes. "Mom," lengthening the sound, half-tender, half-begging, "you worry too much. Stop being overprotective." So I laid off of the inquiry.

Besides, I was mightily distracted. James' depression was particularly bad that spring. In spite of six months of treatment, he still felt terrible, disillusioned with doctors, including me. He couldn't sleep, was jumpy and distracted, and said he couldn't accomplish what he needed to do to prepare his bicycle tours and market them. His desperate rage and fear enveloped me. I tried to appease and assist him, with poor results. In late April, James finally said, "Someone has to tell me what to do, or I'll die." Together we met with his doctor, who recommended a series of electroshocks.

By the second treatment, the depression started to lift rapidly. Still, James was terribly anxious about the impairment of memory that goes with electroconvulsive therapy. His memory eventually came back, but the whole month of May remained a blur. I can barely remember myself how I managed—by doing what most needed to be done at any given moment, relying on my training and years of habit of dealing with crises.

Her father's illness scared Luce. When we met over coffee near the hospital one day, she looked up with a bitter twist to her mouth. "All these years, you and Dad and the doctors, you told me I'd get better. When you're a kid you believe that everything will get better when you grow up. I've always believed in medicine." She shook her head to express the reverse.

I remember my silence, the heaviness in my gut.

"Then I look at Dad. It doesn't really get better when you get older, does it? It gets worse."

I held her hand. We were both crying. I tried, "You are not your father. It will be different." But my heart was not in it, I too had had the stuffing knocked out of me.

James recovered well, completely free of depression by June and bending over crossword puzzles for hours to exercise his memory. Luce seemed better too. I remember one warm evening at our house when she regaled her father, brother, and me with a portrait of "the painter dude."

We sat at the kitchen table that had reunited us since the children were small, from which I could see the setting sun in a glory that gladdened my heart, as it had for countless evenings. The smell of honeysuckle came in through the wide open doors and David's now manly voice alternated with his sister's joyous tones.

Luce spoke as if she recounted a tale. "I walk by the library all the time, right? It's two blocks from my house. So, that day, I come in and one of the guys who works there comes up. He says he is a painter and he's noticed me, and he wants me to model for him." She pouts as if dubious, raises her open hands and shrugs. "I don't know him, never talked to him. He's kind of like an old hippie. Well, not that old, thirty, thirty-five? Skinny. I say, 'I don't know' . . ." Her voice trailed, then sped up. "So he backs up and he says, 'Just think about it. You can tell me later.'"

"What did you do?" asked David, clearly interested.

"Well, I talked to him a few times. He's real nice. I went to his place, it's not bad what he does. So I just sit while he paints, and we talk. He reads a lot and he's okay, just a little weird. I said he doesn't need to pay me but he bought me dinner. Not like he's coming on to me or anything. He's old," stressing the last word. Then she chuckled gently. "It's kind of fun."

Later that evening she said she'd decided she wanted to go back to the university. Did she truly feel better? She sounded excited by the future, not manic but hopeful. Was she really? Or skillful at hiding her fears, as well as her drug use, from parents eager to believe in her recovery? I'll never know.

ALTERNATE REALITY

The summer of 1994 began in a flowering of hope. James felt remarkably good. He focused his energy and intelligence on preparing two bicycle tours for August and September, reading avidly about France. He was again the good companion I had chosen long ago, curious about the world and enthusiastic about a project.

Coming home from work one late afternoon, I found him sitting at a desk covered with open guidebooks. The yellows and reds of unfolded Michelin maps, strewn on the floor, lit up the room.

"Look," he said, eyes smiling at me, clear as a summer sky. "I found this little road along the Loire and a hotel just ten kilometers from Blois. Perfect distance."

He pulled a book closer and pointed to a photo of the hotel. I leaned, my hand resting lightly on his shoulder, to look at it closely. The old house's tall windows opened to a garden and vines covered its walls. "It looks lovely," I said, "like a real family home." Before I became aware of it, my fingers had moved to caress James' neck above his T-shirt collar.

"And check the menu," he said.

We talked leisurely about gastronomic choices. His good humor reminded me of the best of our years together.

Relieved of the burden of worry for him, I too bounced back and could rejoice without restraint for Anna. She'd been living with her partner Rick for a few months now and worked hard in physical therapy to regain strength. Theater, her great love since she was ten years old, put her back at the center of a community of friends. And it focused her concentration, which had been vaporized for months after her accident.

I remember her, alone on stage under a harsh spotlight in a bare cement hall, performing a short play she'd written. Intensity burned in her dark gaze as she gave life to a young New York woman mistreated by police after a rape. Anna's taut body and her voice, holding back emotions at first when she exposed the facts, then poised at the exact point of balance between a shout and a wail, showed us a girl all at once strong and fragile. Glancing around me, I saw I wasn't the only one in tears. When I went around the dusty back curtain at intermission to embrace her, she stiffened and looked angry at the interruption, so focused was she on her character.

She appeared in a succession of leading roles that season, from Portia to Miss Firecracker and Blanche DuBois. Her intelligence for wide-ranging roles and the physicality of her talent blew me away. She moved like a dancer and used the powerful voice inherited from her father like a musical instrument, from viola to trombone. Her dramatic power pulsed into the far corners of the dark theater. After the lights came back on at the end of *A Streetcar Named Desire*, those who'd watched emerged shaken, the loosened emotions written large on their faces as they rose from their seats. Anna was drained and happy when we went backstage to congratulate her.

David, having finished his junior year of high school, celebrated the long summer days by camping with friends and climbing mountains. He came back with stories of the wildlife of the forest and the wild antics of his buddies. For a guy who seemed to survive exclusively on nachos and root beer, he was lean, healthy, and joyous.

Whenever I saw Luce, once or twice a week, she too appeared well with an easy laugh and graceful gestures. But, searching for

memories of her that summer, I come up with wildly discord-
ant scenes. It's as if I'm looking at a triptych. To the left, a panel
with Renaissance portraits of a lovely young woman in summer
dresses, in yellows, pinks, and pale blues. On the right panel, I see
hellish reds and thick shadows, a Bosch-dark scene of pain and
deceit. In the center is the composite picture of all the elements
of the drama as I think I understand it now, with the full range of
shapes and colors of a chaotic reality.

Luce admitted later the double life she led then. She got drunk
often and brought home tough young men I would've been scared
to see her with. She did not visit her best friend from high school
who lived around the corner because she was too ashamed of her
drunkenness and drug use to seek her when she was lonely. Yet, a
year before, she'd taken that same girl's boyfriend to the hospital
after he cut his wrists and then, to spare her friend, cleaned the
blood from their apartment. She helped friends, even strangers,
more than she could help herself.

One afternoon in late June, stepping out of her apartment, she
ran into the brother of the tall, dark boyfriend she'd loved so much
at fifteen. She hadn't seen his brother in years. He was headed two
blocks away, to a drug house. "Come with me. I'll show you the
best thing ever."

There, he gently injected heroin into her vein. "You'll see, you'll
love it."

"He was right, Mom," she told me much later. "It was the first
time in my life I felt normal—happy, not depressed."

Yet she stayed away from heroin for a whole month. She even
told her psychiatrist that she'd tried heroin once but would never
use it again because she knew it was too dangerous. But then she
did. She went back to the drug house in August, convincing herself—the sadly typical addict's self-delusion—that she could have
a summer fling with heroin, that she would take it only sometimes,
for fun, and stop when university classes began in September.

I felt a searing flash of anger when I heard this. Three people knew about her drug use when we didn't. The boy who'd led
her to heroin the first time wouldn't tell, of course. His world,

into which he had just invited Luce, had its own perceptions and rules, where family didn't count. But Luce? She knew the danger yet didn't seek our help. And the psychiatrist? I would have loved to point fingers, assign blame to someone else to free myself from guilt over not guessing the truth. As if I could, should, have guessed. Which is not a rational thought, yet it still has a tenacious hold on me.

But, now, I can no longer judge my daughter. I was angry at her choices, I have called her a fool, fought and pleaded with her, but I have immense compassion for the hold that the intractable suffering of depression had on her being. She chose a dismal solution in an attempt to wipe out an unbearable reality. She gave up hope for any other source of relief, and certainly for psychiatric treatment. "Let's face it, Mom," she told me later, "the legal drugs weren't doing anything for me. I still felt like shit all the time." She didn't turn either toward the higher power of the Twelve-Step program that had kept her sober for a long time, nor to her fellows in recovery.

Later, once we could talk about this, she gave me a sharp-edged small rock, dark and heavy, black-brown with hues of rust catching the light. Light and shadow revealed fine striations densely packed parallel to the rock's longer side.

"Look at these," she said, "up close. Don't they look like bars? Like the bars of a prison? The prison has shrunk and the bars have come closer and closer. I am caught inside and I've shrunk too. Or I've been crushed slowly. Now I can't move, I can't feel, I can't even see out.

"You know," she added in a thin faraway voice, looking at the rock in my palm, then at the tears in my eyes, "I know people love me. They say it and I believe them. But I can't feel it. As if it can't get in."

I have kept the rock.

I have compassion, too, for the professional helpers, including me, and her fellows in recovery, like her father, who could not reach her petrified soul.

When her psychiatrist told me, much later, that in July Luce had mentioned trying heroin once, I pulled back as if slapped. I was hurt, angry, and confused. The doctor, a trusting young woman who mustn't have personally known many junkies, inquired repeatedly in the following months if Luce had used heroin again, and Luce convinced her that she would never repeat that experience. She kept to herself what a revelation it had been, that something could relieve her of pain in a way nothing else had and, she was convinced, nothing else could.

By the time we learned of her heroin use, much too late, she was hooked. Would things have been different if the doctor had intervened immediately after the first try? What could she have done, what else would I have done in her place? Should she have told me? We were colleagues, but she was bound by confidentiality. Anyone who has treated young adults knows the importance and the challenge of keeping lines of communication clear. For the doctor to talk to me about her, Luce had to invite me to join them. In any case, what leverage would anybody have had then to force Luce into drug treatment when obviously she had no intention of being clean and sober? When she'd been successfully hiding her drinking and drug use for months?

She hoodwinked her psychiatrist, not showing up for appointments when she was high or hung over, then lying her way through the next session. Her father and I were just as blind. And she lied, as any addict does. Addiction is "cunning, baffling, powerful," says the Big Book of AA.

In August, Luce went for a weekend visit to a friend. This was her oldest friend, whose house had been her second home in grade school, the one she used to dance with at fourteen at the swimming hole, the one with whom she planned to practice after medical school. When Luce arrived, her friend thought she looked ill, too thin and vague, and asked pointed questions about drugs and depression, which Luce evaded.

The "painter dude" for whom Luce modeled took a series of photos of her during the summer to prepare for his paintings. They show a remarkable array of moods. In close-ups where her smile is heartbreakingly innocent, she looks very young. Others show a mature beauty who looks back over her shoulder, head high on a slender neck and thick hair brushed back, with an air of knowing far too much about the world in her level gaze. I recognize the complex young woman, one day cynical, harsh in her judgment of society and advocating anarchy to force it open, another day the idealist who wanted to relieve the pains of war and poverty with Doctors Without Borders.

In one photo she wears a flowered summer dress and moves forward with a grin, as if she didn't have a care in the world. I fiercely want to embrace this girl, to feel her slender waist bend and hear her ticklish giggle as I hug her tight.

That open, trusting image was already a mirage. When I called to see Luce during the summer, she did not tell me that she was in trouble. She found reasons—had to work . . . met a friend—to cancel our dates before finally accepting a drive with David and me in late August.

James had left for France to lead bicycle groups. I planned to join him for three weeks after the tours, in September, taking Anna to celebrate her return to health with our French family. James and I had discussed whether I should stay home for Luce's sake, but she convinced us that she'd be okay on her own. She would start classes at the university and promised to drop by our house so that David wouldn't be lonely. Still, I couldn't shake a nagging worry that depression would again seize her.

David and Luce had long liked spending time together. Many of my best memories show us, with or without the dog, at the beach, a river, or hot springs. As if to affirm our common history of happiness, I was determined to enjoy the late summer with them. Luce and I reached a compromise: she agreed on a date and I promised not to show up before noon.

I gave her until one o'clock before pulling in front of her apartment. David went to knock on her door. Her face looked slack, barely awake as she came out, but brightened into a smile when she saw me at the wheel of James' red convertible. I was pleased, having thought it would be festive to ride with the top down. I drove toward the mountains and repeatedly glanced at Luce, who sat next to me. Hair swirling around her head, eyes closed, and a lazy smile on her lips, she seemed content, happy, I hoped. The wind stole away words, so we remained quiet. I patted her hand and she held mine for a moment in return.

The sky was very clear and I decided to go to a fire lookout, high above the Cascades foothills with a view of the coastal chain. The low-slung convertible was not adapted to the logging road we climbed and I bumped the chassis a couple of times.

"Wow, Mom," David said, "you're going to hurt Dad's car."

"His precious car. He isn't going to be happy," added Luce.

The kids' criticism was good-hearted and I laughed. "You're right, I'd better be careful," and slowed to a crawl. I delighted in being with them in the open air, in the sun, in the wilderness. I teased Luce that she was as pale as a mushroom and needed to leave her cave. The memory of her easy, throaty laugh seizes me with longing. It made me high on hope for her.

Pink wild rhododendrons were still in bloom at high elevation, skinny bushes beneath giant firs. We stopped to walk among the flowers in a glorious gold light slanting through the trees, then hiked to the fire lookout set in a small meadow at the very top of a ridge.

I stood in one spot, slowly turning my body around to take in the sight of the immense sky, ridge after ridge of blue mountains, and precipitous valleys, deep and dark. Beauty filled me and I floated in grateful wonder. Fearing that Luce might be unhappy although she pretended not to be, I extended my arm, offering her the world. "Regarde, chérie. Isn't this beautiful?"

She raised a hand to stop me. "Mom." Her tone was dry, dispassionate. "I know this makes you happy. But it doesn't work for me. I can't see what you talk about. For me mountains are only green furry bumps." I kept forgetting how little she could see. She did not complain, she was sweet about it, so gentle that it pained me. She let me hold her, say I was sorry.

I remember our bittersweet mood after coming down from the mountain, and jokes about the waitress' ruffled skirt, too short for middle-age legs, when we stopped for pancakes in a logging town. "What you have to do for a job," sighed Luce, shaking her head.

She looked happy that day. Maybe she was high, and that's what made her loose and relaxed. I don't care.

Then I left. I left her. That evening, at the door of her dark apartment, and a few days later when I flew off to France. I'll forever regret it. I don't know if it would have made a difference. I'll never know. I wish I did.

Sweet Assassin

W hen James and I returned home in October, all seemed
in good order. David was even taller, healthy, and keeping up with his schoolwork. Anna reunited with her boyfriend
Rick in their apartment. The house was intact, the phone beeping
with mundane messages, the cat and dog happy. We invited Luce
to an early dinner at home the day after our return. James drove
to pick her up because bad night vision didn't allow her to ride
her scooter at night. When they returned, he went straight to his
office at the back of the house to open mail.

I stopped dicing vegetables when I heard the door close.
Anticipation lifted my heart as I rinsed and dried my hands, and
I walked toward Luce's footsteps in the corridor, the sooner to
embrace her. I stopped in my tracks when I saw her, hit by the
thought that something terrible had happened. She moved slowly,
her face sagging around a phony smile.

She'd lost weight and gone from slender to skinny, her skin was
off-color, pale and greenish. "Luce, what's wrong?" I asked as I
held her. Then, touching her cheek softly with my fingertips, "Are
you sick?"

She straightened her shoulders and pulled away. "I'm all right,"
she said, without inflection. The cold hardness in her voice made
me back off.

I turned on the stove and poured oil in a skillet. Water droplets sputtered when I scooped vegetables into the hot oil, the only sound for a while as I gathered my thoughts. David had come in from his bedroom and, after they greeted each other with a kiss on the cheek, Luce led him to sit across from me. Having the children perch on the bar stools on the other side of the kitchen island while I cooked had always been a pleasure. I took Luce's choice as a gift, a balm, and started speaking again, asking her questions about the previous three weeks.

She made a visible effort to gather up energy and appear animated, looking straight at me, but her eyes soon slid off my face and she hunched over, elbows on the counter. Her reluctant answers to my questions, spoken in a monotone, began to paint a scary picture, at once familiar and confusing.

"Yes, I signed up for classes."—"No, I haven't gone."—"I don't want to explain now, I'll tell you later."—"Soon."—"No, I'm not sick. Not depressed."—"What do I do? Not much. I see friends." This did not make sense. "I'm all right, I'll tell you."

Oh, no, I thought, not again. How many times had her plans for school been crushed? What were we going to do? Steam rising from the pan obscured Luce's expression and a similar daze spread over my mind. I noticed that David kept his head down and his expression blank, a talent he'd perfected over the last few years. I asked him to set the table while I finished preparing the meal. I swayed, as if I could fall at any moment, and wondered how much jetlag contributed to this. I spread both palms on the counter, looked up at the wall clock and automatically added nine hours for the time difference between home and Paris. It was three a.m. for my body. No wonder I feel woozy, I thought, as if to discount my sense of dread. But I knew better.

I called James and we sat down to dinner. The organic smoothness of the old wood table, a distant ridgeline against the rose-tinted western sky that I admired most evenings, the weight of a full water glass, those familiar sensations anchored and appeased me. Maybe this could be just an ordinary congenial family dinner.

Luce asked how her French cousins were, and kept the conversation bouncy. She told stories of the last three weeks, distracting us with her usual humor about playing with the dog one day in a park, about old friends we knew, about the painter dude. She was showing off, as if saying, "Look, I am not depressed, I have fun and I do things." The final message was, "Get off my back!"

James and I went along and told our own stories of our time in France. But I kept watching Luce with disquiet. After a while I saw, sitting across the table from her, that she could literally no longer keep her eyes straight. Those gorgeous eyes, bright as gems, which had caused her so much pain and us so much concern. As she looked at me, one eye remained aimed at my face while the other roamed upward, then sideways, as if she were under anesthesia.

I sprang up to go to her, my voice loud and croaking. "What's happening? What drug are you on?" She stood to evade me, backing up to the wall.

"Nothing. I'm not on drugs." She sounded both defiant and pleading.

My eye caught a movement as David looked up at her, his eyes wide. Was he surprised? I wondered. He blushed, then bent his head down and shrank in his chair, looking much smaller and younger.

I didn't touch Luce but pressed on: "I don't believe you. You're under the influence. If not that, you're very sick."

She grabbed the heavy, metal-studded black leather jacket she wore all the time then, a motorcycle-cop uniform a friend had given her. "Dad, will you take me home please?"

I cleaned the kitchen on autopilot, all the while replaying the scene in my mind. David helped me in silence, his movements as slow and deliberate as mine, it seemed. I was grateful he didn't retreat to his room.

When James came back twenty minutes later, he slammed the door. His words were hot and his eyes fierce as he faced me, his face very close to mine. "She's an adult, you can't treat her like that. You'll only push her away."

I flinched, but held my ground, dug in like a bull. "I'm sure she is on something."

"Can't you trust people? She told you she is not doing drugs."

"You didn't see? Her eyes were going all over the place. I tell you, if it's not drugs, there is something else terribly wrong. Could be neurological. I can't pretend that I don't see what I see. I'm worried."

"Then you need to go to your support group and get off other people's backs."

We were sliding into dangerous, sickly familiar territory. I stopped talking. I wanted to cry, but I also wanted to act. I breathed deeply, head low, stubborn, not looking into James' eyes to tell him, "We'll have to disagree on that. It may be a mistake, but I can't not do it. I'll go to Luce's tomorrow morning and take her to the lab."

James snorted, but said nothing.

Then David spoke. He'd hung at the edge of our dispute. "She came up here when you were away," he said in a low, reluctant voice. "One day she brought a friend, a guy I don't know. I saw him, in your bathroom, he was shooting up." He paused. We both stared at him, dumbstruck. "He offered Luce some, but she said 'Not here.' And then they left."

It was obviously very hard for David to break the sibling's covenant of not telling Mom and Dad on your sister. "I thought you needed to know," he said.

I sat down at the kitchen table. A terrible weight pinned me to the chair and I had to lean on the table. I began to cry.

James also looked stricken. "We'll go tomorrow," he said.

We went together to Luce's apartment the next morning. I thought it was a sad place, in a cheap clapboard building painted a dull brown. Her scooter was parked at the bottom of two steps leading to a small wooden deck in front of her door. We knocked and waited in the wet gray air. I had called around nine o'clock to tell her we were coming and she'd agreed, but it still took her a long time to come to the door.

It opened directly onto a square room, the only window covered by a blind. The room darkened as soon as we shut the door behind us. Luce was barefoot with a dress on. She walked back to her bed after stubbing her cigarette in an ashtray.

The queen-size bed took up most of the room, with black flan-
nel sheets that did not reflect the light of a small reading lamp.
Luce and I sat on her bed, James in the only chair. The sheets held
the smell of incense, tobacco, and cold candle wax. She looked
sleepy and weak, and leaned against her pillows. Her eyes closed
and it seemed to take great effort for her to reopen them when I
spoke.

"Luce, I want to take you to the lab and run some tests." I
was concerned that she might refuse and, being legally an adult,
couldn't be forced.

"But I'm okay," she protested feebly.

I took her hand. "You are not okay. You look very sick." Words
caught on my fear as on barbed wire. "Either it's drugs and we
need to know, or it's an illness, and we need to know that too."

I looked at James, his face pale, nose pinched and mouth partly
open, blue eyes gone gray. He leaned toward his daughter. "We
need to do something. You need help."

"I'm okay," she repeated in a lusterless voice.

"Let's go," I urged, but gently, as with a sick person. "Put shoes
on." I picked up her jacket off the floor, laid it on the bed next
to her. She only looked up at James, then me, not moving. I slid
an arm behind her shoulders to help her sit up. James brought
her shoes and put them on her feet with tender gestures, as he
had when she was small. I helped her with her coat and, his arm
around her waist, James walked her out the door, down the steps,
and to the car. She seemed to move without personal will, a numb
automaton.

She woke up enough when we arrived at the laboratory to walk
in by herself and then go from the waiting room to the collection
cubicle. After that we took her to our home to wait for the results.
I had requested to be called as soon as possible. Luce lay down on
the living room couch and was soon asleep.

I don't know what I did while waiting for the lab's call. I had just
come back from three weeks away and did not schedule patients
the first couple of days after a trip to Europe because of jet lag. I
probably called my answering service, and might have gone to the

office to pick up mail and consult the appointment book—telling myself that we'd been through all this before. Luce would get better. It would be all right.

This time, though, it was very bad. The concentration of opiates in Luce's blood was so high that, had she not been habituated to them, she would have been in a coma. She'd looked sleepy when we met her at the apartment, yet she had stood upright and climbed unassisted the stairs to the lab. When I got the results, an hour or so later, I told all this to James in a few words and we went to her. I was moved by despair, fear, and anger as much as by the need to help her.

I shook her gently until she woke and sat up, rubbing her eyes and passing a hand through the thick hair that fell over her face. Her brow wrinkled as she squinted her eyes to focus on me. It took her only a glance to read my expression and she turned her head away, her face now a wooden mask of unconcern.

I sat down at the other end of the couch. "Do you know what this tells me?" I asked, wanting but not daring to touch her, as if I feared she would bolt.

She remained silent, eyes fixed on the midday sky through the window. James stood nearby rod-straight, knees locked and arms folded tight around his chest, as if he needed to contain his heart.

"It tells me that you are on high doses of heroin, that you probably shot up just before we came this morning, and that you've acquired tolerance." I stopped, exhausted by the meaning of my own words. She didn't move. "Which means that you've been using for some time." I paused. No response. "Luce," her name flew forcefully from my lips, "you can't lie anymore. Tell us."

Finally, her defiant posture thawed and she began talking. Mumbled words, long gaps, a few clear sentences, some rambling ones that expired without making a point. James, who'd been standing, folded as if hit behind the knees and sat facing her. He and I exchanged glances at times, but mostly listened, hunched under the weight of what we heard.

I can't recall precisely what she said then, or the questions James and I asked. More details would come out in the next few days, but the story began to take shape right there, in the cold dim living room where no one thought of turning on the lights or lighting a fire. She said she'd used heroin every day from August until now, mid-October. She'd tried to stop when classes began in September but wasn't able to.

It must have been to comfort myself that I resorted to familiar medical acts. Luce let me look at her arms to check for infection at the injection sites and I made a mental note to schedule an HIV test. Devastating thoughts, yet I felt stronger with this façade of control.

But it soon gave way and I was thoroughly undone. "How could you?" I wailed. "You know everything about drugs. You've been in recovery groups for years. You know what heroin does to people. You've been a peer counselor at the university. How could you?" I stamped my foot in frustration.

"When I did it, I felt good. Not depressed. Happy. Normal."

"But sweetie," I begged, "it's so dangerous."

Anger flared on her face and she stared me down. "Look, Mom, I—don't—care. I feel bad all the time. The psychiatric drugs don't work, let's face it, they don't work for me."

My mouth opened for a retort but none came, so I closed it to swallow the bitter truth. The previous years had shown Luce was correct. Her psychiatrists tried to find a new medicine that would work better than the last one, or mucked around with dosages. The hospital psychiatrist, at the end of the inpatient stay in 1991, had confided to the local doctor who now followed Luce that she had one of the most severe forms of adolescent bipolar disorders she'd seen. Neither doctor had used those words in front of me, and I hadn't dared to predict an outcome for my daughter. I had strained to leave diagnosis and prognosis to them, to act and think as a mother. I must have feared that the specter of all that could go wrong with such an illness would paralyze me and I clung to the urging from the hospital psychiatrist. "We'll do all we can. But you are her mother. As long as she is alive you can't give up."

Shaken by Luce's angry words, I recalled when, a few months before—Luce lived at our house and didn't do drugs—her local psychiatrist had indicated during a joint meeting that she couldn't quite assess how Luce's body processed lithium or antidepressants. Her chemistry seemed out of whack, unpredictable.

Now, in a room that held memories of happy family traditions, family legacy acquired a new meaning. Luce looked at me straight on. "It really sucks. I get the manic-depressive gene from you, and the weird drug reactions from Dad. You said doctors would find new stuff that worked." Her mouth took a bitter turn, her voice a sharp tone, and she shook her head. "I don't believe it anymore. It only gets worse." Anger set her face hard. Then she turned away, coiled her body into a tight ball in the corner of the couch, and closed her eyes. She was soon asleep.

James and I sought refuge at the kitchen table, the heart of the house. The room felt cold without heat from the stove or cooking smells. I couldn't remember when I'd last eaten and didn't believe I'd ever be hungry again.

We went around and around possible options. There were few at this point. We should intervene immediately to get Luce away from heroin. Only after that was accomplished could one devise a long-term plan of action. First she must be safe and our house was not; she could get away when the craving took her, as we knew it would. The local drug treatment center, with its open door policy, wasn't secure either. We agreed I should consult Luce's psychiatrist.

The psychiatrist cried out, "No!" in the phone when I gave her the news, then asked breathless questions. Later, in a calmer voice, she listed the local resources and decided she would request from the court that Luce be committed to the County Psychiatric Hospital, a secure facility by the jail, on the grounds that she was a danger to herself. When I put her on hold to ask James, he consented. "At least she'll be safe," he said quietly. I nodded. Having both worked in psychiatric hospitals, we didn't believe we'd be sending our daughter to the set of *One Flew over the Cuckoo's Nest.* I thanked my colleague, relieved that she'd carry part of the burden. We were so tired.

The judge granted the request and ordered that Luce be assigned for five days to the hospital. All this was done in a matter of a few hours, so Luce was still under the influence, looking relaxed when I woke her up to announce where we'd take her. She did not resist, and James drove us to the locked unit. I sat next to her on the back seat, holding her hand, the three of us silent.

Coming out of the car, I saw long brick walls topped with razor wire glinting in the afternoon light. We passed by the entrance to the jail, with its armed guards, and found the door to the psychiatric ward. In a small airless anteroom, a poster by a wall phone displayed rules to identify ourselves. We followed the steps and an inner door opened to admit us into a long resonant space where sounds of loud voices, clanging metal doors, and chairs dragged on the concrete floor reverberated against the hard walls. The din hit me like a shock wave.

Dark brick everywhere, neon lights, a little daylight from high clerestory windows. The nursing station was at the center of the long rectangular room and individual cubicles with open metal doors ran along two walls, each of them a cell with a metal platform for a bed. On either side of the nursing station in the central open area, patients sat, watched TV, or paced and smoked. Most looked lost and pathetic, like homeless schizophrenics. Others very tough, the street junkies. Each seemed confined in a coffin-shaped space of extreme loneliness. I had the shocking thought, when a nurse took charge of Luce and led her to one of the cells, that Luce looked as if she belonged there, much too thin, her narrow back tense, looking straight ahead without any acknowledgment of the others or of the place.

James and I met with a social worker in a small office close to the entrance to give her a history of Luce's troubles. She seemed to understand the danger of suicide in addition to the need for detox. After this meeting and a quick good-bye to Luce, back in the car James and I told each other that, as scary as it looked, this place might be the best for her, considering the lack of treatment facilities in our state that serve people afflicted with a mental illness combined with addiction. Still, my heart felt frozen solid.

I can barely imagine how we lived through the next week and how I could work. Every morning I drove to my office with extra caution, knowing I was distracted. I arrived early enough to have time to read the charts of patients scheduled that day, because I didn't trust my memory. Before each appointment I breathed deeply and meditated a few minutes to center my attention. I took copious notes, afraid that I might later forget something a patient had said or a medication I had prescribed, and I wrote down lists of phone calls to return and tasks to remember.

James joined me at the office in late afternoon and we went together a few blocks away to the jail. Administratively, the psychiatric hospital was separate from the prison, but my feeling was that we visited our daughter in jail. The neon lights and the clanking sounds and rough voices resonating off the brick walls created a jarring atmosphere.

Luce looked weak, unable to eat and barely able to stand for the first two or three days, shaky and cold from withdrawal, sullen and silent. She seemed lost to us, her situation hopeless. Only the sturdy support of the social worker, who gave us information every day when we came to visit, and our determined stubbornness kept us going. The psychiatric director of the place never even talked to us, convinced, he told someone else, that Luce was the spoiled brat of overindulgent parents and that all she needed was "tough love" and to be told to shape up. He apparently didn't bother to read the report from the 1991 hospitalization, which I had brought, or to listen to the social worker. It was an ordeal to go there.

During our visits, Luce hardly spoke beyond the words "I'm fine." But when Anna came by herself one day, Luce told her, "Mom and Dad have spent so much time, energy and money keeping me alive. Why don't they just give up?" Anna kept that comment to herself at the time, just as Luce kept to herself her plan to get released and then kill herself.

I don't know what to make of something the head nurse told

me several years later: "I remember Luce because there was a glow to her that other patients missed. It was intelligence, but it was also life, the life force." I often saw that glow in Luce, coming from her heart, guts and brains, and her humor, irrepressibly expressed in dance, daring, kisses, or laughter. Yet I'm still surprised that it could be visible to a stranger at such a time.

After the worst of her withdrawal symptoms receded, Luce started eating and talking to a counselor. She said she was better, much better, and that she intended to stay clean. No, she said, she didn't need to go to Sobriety First for inpatient treatment of her addiction, as the staff recommended. She would work with her sponsor, get a job, and get her life back together. No, she had no intention of living at home, she would pay for her apartment herself with her job. She had a plan.

The three of us sat at the far end of the common room at the next visit when she presented her plan to her dad and me. She smiled broadly but couldn't quite pull off her charm offensive. Was she less effective at lying or were we finally less gullible? We told her the plan was crazily dangerous, and she walked away from us.

The social worker noticed our distress and invited us into her windowless office. A tall woman in earth-toned loose clothes, she looked caged in the small space. She glanced up at a potted plant hung in a corner, as if greenery could refresh her.

James blurted out, "This so-called plan of Luce's is totally insane. She'll be a sitting duck. She could die out there." His hands flew up, encompassing the whole world, full of horrid possibilities.

The therapist nodded. "I'm sure she's lying and I agree that she's a suicidal risk." She grimaced and let out an exasperated sigh. "But she is very smart, she knows the lingo, and she sounds real good. She'll answer all the judge's questions the correct way, and he won't commit her to further treatment."

I needed to leave, fast. Impotent anger and fear swirled in my gut.

The next day, the last that the judge had ordered Luce to be held involuntarily, the medical director decided to not even seek a judge's order for extended commitment to his facility. For that, the doctor would have to demonstrate that Luce's behavior showed that she was an immediate danger to herself or others. Laws to protect patients' individual rights are very clear that such is the criterion for holding a person against his or her will. The hospital was only set up to deal with the immediate, life-threatening symptoms of acute withdrawal.

So the doctor discharged Luce but strongly recommended to her that she should go voluntarily to Sobriety First to treat her addiction. Then he added, which was true, that nobody could force her to do so without a judge's decision. When a nurse reported this to me, I was too numb to argue, too shocked to trust my gut feeling that Luce was indeed a danger to herself or question the director's judgment.

James and I left the unit with Luce and walked together to our car. One after the other, her father and I begged her to come home—better yet, to go for drug treatment. At the end of his rope, James told her that he wouldn't support her living alone in her apartment, that it was a recipe for relapse.

She was stubborn and flippant. "You don't need to support me if you don't agree. But I'll do what I plan to do anyway." She had the legal right to do just that and we were powerless to convince her. No argument, suggestion, or begging penetrated her armor. James and I held hands in shared misery, watching our daughter walk away in the cold with her little suitcase.

So she was on her own again, nineteen years old and shaky. Later she told Anna that she bought a gun the first day out of the hospital and hid it in her apartment. She never called a sponsor but instead found heroin right away. We discovered later that, not having money to pay, she told her Mexican connection, José, that she would deal for him.

She pulled herself together just enough to call us once a day, saying that no, she did not want any visit, she was fine. But Anna and Rick, stopping by her apartment, found the door unlocked and discovered Luce, dress muddied from falling in an alley, passed out on her bed. A man knocked on the door and then slunk away when Rick, broad-shouldered and six-foot-three, opened.

Anna and Rick were scared, wondering if they should tell us: They decided not to in order to keep a connection to Luce, tenuous as it might be. A few months before, Luce had for the first time in her life exploded in anger at Anna, ranting for minutes on end that Anna didn't care for her. The next day, when Anna asked her to explain, Luce had no recollection of her outburst. So Anna had been cautious about crossing her sister ever since.

Luce went down fast, in a matter of days, using the drugs she was supposed to be selling. One evening, stopping at her place after work, I found her in tears. She admitted she was in terrible shape, that she was going to die if she didn't stop. She gathered a few clothes and I brought her home.

There, James held her close to his heart while I called Sobriety First to arrange for admission. I was told we couldn't bring her right then unless we could write a check for the total cost of the four-week program because our insurance policy didn't cover it. I answered I'd have to get a loan at our bank first thing in the morning and bring the papers with us. I don't remember being mad or disgusted; this was how things were.

Following the call to Sobriety First, we sat together for dinner. James, David, and I lingered at the table longer than usual, without needing to plan it, because we wanted to surround Luce with everyday words and gestures. After a while, she rose to make a phone call, speaking a few indistinct words, then came back to sit at the table. James had noticed how antsy she was and when, after a while, she grabbed her leather jacket and said, "I'm going out for a cigarette," he sensed danger.

"She usually goes to the deck in back to smoke, not to the front door," he explained later. He rushed out. She had her coat on and was walking down our long driveway toward an idling car. James ran and tackled her. She fought him but, when the car sped away, she collapsed in his arms and he rocked her for a long time. The man in the car was her dealer, she admitted through her tears.

Sobriety First was familiar to me. For years I'd worked there as a consultant. Looking like a family home from the outside, it revealed its institutional character by the dark linoleum in the large foyer, the clang of metal trays and wafts of overcooked food in steam containers from the cafeteria to the right. Patients in sweat pants and an assortment of sad faces filed in for breakfast.

I went left to the receptionist's window and addressed her by name. "Morning, Dr. Campion," she answered. "Who are you seeing today? I don't have you on the schedule."

Tears came up, with a sour mixture of shame and self-pity that shamed me some more. Did I think I was any better than those patients and their families, that I deserved to be spared? By virtue of what? I knew better, except that, deep down, I must have hoped that all the energy I had spent battling addiction and mental illness for years would count in my favor. As if I could bargain with fate, buy protection with my contributions. But destiny is crueler than any mafia goon.

I stepped aside to show Luce and James. "This is my daughter. Her dad and I are here to admit her."

"I'll call the counselor and he'll meet you in the exam room," the receptionist said without missing a beat. "You know the way." Soon Luce was led upstairs to her room.

Luce's psychiatrist had agreed to join the staff meeting at Sobriety First to address the risk of suicide. James and I came into the meeting room after signing admission papers and being informed of the rules of the place. We took seats along the dark wood table and, looking at many known faces, I felt the now painfully familiar imbalance from having my feet, as it were, in two different domains. In one I was considered an expert, in the other I had no certainty, no clue even on this particular day, on how any decision would impact my daughter's long-term well-being, possibly her life. I heard silence, in contrast to the usual small talk that precedes staff meetings, and noticed lowered gazes, hands nervously toying with coffee cups and pens. I guessed that the doctors, nurses, and counselors in this room might also be uncomfortable with my twin roles, so I too lowered my eyes. My hands trembled and I covered one with the other to stop that.

The moment passed and soon the discussion took on speed

and depth. Luce's psychiatrist described her depressive troughs and suicide attempts, then recoveries. She also explained Luce's response to medications. It struck me that we might not know the reality about that, if Luce hadn't taken her meds. Having discovered how much she'd lied in the past few months, I wouldn't put it past her to have stopped taking them. The psychiatrist concluded that the danger of suicide was real and asked how the staff would address it since the facility had no locked doors.

I didn't speak, the better to hear what would be said, and looked at James, whose mouth was tightly shut too. His eyes stared at the blank wall in front of him and appeared to see nothing.

A nurse explained that Luce would be under close observation on a special closed unit for the first days of withdrawal. And her treatment with lithium and antidepressants would be monitored, added the medical director. Only later would she be moved to a regular room to follow a program of lectures and counseling.

It wasn't spelled out in so many words, but the point was that Luce could then leave at any time, to shoot heroin or harm herself in other ways. There was no locked security room, as in a psychiatric unit. We'd have to deal with this situation later, when she'd leave the supervised nursing section.

The discussion then rebounded in another direction. Psychiatric units were equipped to deal with suicidal risk, said an alcoholism counselor, but they did not provide specialized treatment for addiction. Heads nodded when he pointed that Luce's depression couldn't be adequately treated while, by shooting up, she chose a dangerous form of escape. Frustration in front of such a conundrum was clear on many faces and people squirmed in their seats.

"How about methadone?" said someone, I forget who. Another debate followed, with pros and cons. In the end, because Luce had used heroin regularly for less than three months, it seemed better for her to aim for complete abstinence rather than substitute another addictive substance.

I would later learn that the friend whom Luce called "the

painter dude" had, around that time, wanted to take her to the local methadone clinic. She'd showed up at his place, so obviously stoned that he got the truth out of her. But she left as soon as he suggested that they go together to the clinic. He called anyway to make an appointment, intending to find Luce afterwards and convince her to come with him. "There is such a long waiting list," he was told, "we couldn't possibly see your friend before two months at the earliest."

James and I left the meeting exhausted. We were back facing the same impossible situation as when Luce was in the psych hospital by the jail. There was no treatment institution in the state for what's called "dual diagnosis," the combination of severe psychiatric and addictive illnesses, and only a handful in the whole country. At home, we continued to rehash the alternatives. We considered the hospital in Kansas where I had trained. It was an exceptional place where patients with complex disorders could stay for months and receive multifaceted care. I knew it to be excellent, and very expensive. Without insurance to help pay, we'd be bankrupt in no time, an irresponsible choice with two other children.

It seemed we ought to give Sobriety First a try. The nurses, with the compassion and loyalty brought forth by our years of working together, promised to take special care of Luce. Several counselors were also friends of James' from recovery meetings. We could visit Luce every day. Her psychiatrist would continue to monitor the medications necessary for her bipolar illness. And we might all get lucky. Anyone who's attended recovery groups knows personally some "walking fucking miracle" as they say, people whose history should logically have led to complete degradation and death, and who now have full satisfying lives. The old dance between fear and hope started again.

Luce's treatment at Sobriety First was supposed to last four weeks, starting October 29, 1994. We told her that we'd give notice to her landlady and move her belongings back home. Where she should live after treatment would be decided later.

I vividly remember that Saturday afternoon in her apartment. I had planned to clean up and pack her stuff so James and David could move it the next day. There were the tussled black bedclothes, candles and incense, now scentless in the cold air, cassette tapes on the floor by the head of the bed, and her silver rings in an ashtray.

In the bathroom I found unused bottles of lithium and antidepressants from the last two months. I was annoyed, but not really surprised. Luce was not the first person I knew to stop taking medication without informing the prescribing doctor. Many of my own patients had.

But what I discovered in the kitchen triggered a rush of fresh horror, as if I'd almost put out of my mind the reality of Luce's heroin use. By the sink that held only a dirty coffee cup was a whole drawer full of syringes with, in the back, powder packets and a small notebook with first names and phone numbers. I stared, frozen, painful breaths expelled as sighing moans.

I jumped when the phone rang and it took me a few frantic seconds to locate it under a sheet. A man with a thick Hispanic accent told me that Luce owed him 450 dollars and that he must be paid, by me if not by her. I wondered if he'd been watching the place and seen me come in. I turned to stare through the window but the visible space held no one. The man told me where to leave an envelope with the money, the next day at the latest. I can't recall if I said even one word in response before he hung up. When I try to remember, a rushing sound fills my ears and a burning flush invades my cheeks, as happened back then.

I emptied the drawer into a brown grocery bag, called James, and in a few frenzied words told him what happened and asked him to join me at the police station.

Being there was another first. The gruff "What d'you want?" from a frazzled-looking receptionist made me want to flee, and I had to steel myself to stay in the cold waiting room where every sound echoed. I repeated in my head, like a mantra, that I needed advice only these people could give in order to respond to the situation and best protect Luce.

James arrived just before we were directed to an office deep inside the building. There, a uniformed officer sat at a desk littered with forms and folders and gestured for us to take a seat. He looked tired and bored as he listened to our story, asked a few questions, rummaged through the paper bag, then set it in a corner and leafed through the address book. That seemed to interest him. "I know those names," he murmured, "and the numbers. So she's dealing for them. That José is a real bad guy, Mexican cartel."

I realize now that Luce hadn't yet told us she was dealing. I asked: "What will they do to our daughter if she doesn't pay?"

He looked up at me as if to consider whether to answer. "It might be anything." His stony stare said it all.

I went cold. "Is it okay if we pay? We won't be in trouble with the law or something?"

"She'd be safer that way. That's what I'd do if it was my daughter." His voice had remained flat, almost mechanical, but suddenly he became human and passion underscored his next statement. "Tell her to stay away from that crowd." And I thought he might indeed have a daughter when our gazes held each other for a moment.

James and I left, haunted by visions of what sociopathic drug dealers could do to Luce. Would they look for her at our house, where one of them had driven the night before. Could they hurt David? Fear spiraled. We decided fast that we'd pay up. We pooled all the cash we had, got more at the ATM, and dropped it where the man had told me to, under a hedge not far from Luce's apartment. Then James went home and I drove to Sobriety First to see Luce.

I barged into her room, not even stopping by the nurse's station to check in. She was alone, writing in a notebook, and surprise wrinkled her brow. I was furious, anger fueled by panic. "Luce, you're really out of it. Where was your head? Selling drugs, for God's sake. Did you think you could deal with criminals and not get hurt?"

She dismissed the comment with a shrug of the shoulders. But just a small shrug. In fact, she looked scared.

"What were you thinking?"

"I wasn't thinking."

"That's for sure. Creeps like that have no consideration for you. They'll use you and that's all. You're so stoned that you can't even deal, you can't work, and they want their money. The only thing you have is you're young and you've got a beautiful body. They'll take it and they'll sell it."

She cringed and started crying. I calmed down, sat by her, and let my own tears flow. "I can't believe that you would deal, that you would spread the poison to other kids. It makes me sick. It's not like you. What's happened to you?"

"I'm really fucked up, Mom. I want to quit. I want to get back to being me."

But she couldn't quit, not quite yet. After five days at Sobriety First, she ran away, we didn't know where. James called the policeman we'd met. "I know you can't do anything, no crime has been committed. But could you spread the word? If any officer sees her stoned, in an alley somewhere, have them call us?"

"Can I come to your house for a photo?"

That was November 3rd, David's seventeenth birthday. We'd invited a few of his friends for dinner and he was trying to be as bright as he could. Then a cop showed up to talk about his sister. David cursed under his breath. "That's one more birthday Luce has ruined for me." It was true; she often fell apart right around that time, a few days before her own birthday. He loved her, but it was exhausting for him too, to be dragged to a hospital, pushed into family therapy, or simply left alone with his own fears while his parents ran around frantically.

Luce was on the streets for her birthday, November 7th. She'd called home the evening before and David answered. He arranged to see her for coffee before starting school the next morning and held the phone up to his father. James was too angry to talk to her or see her. "I sure don't see what there is to celebrate about this birthday," he muttered, handing me the phone. "She's screwing up her life."

Luce agreed to meet me for lunch at a deli close to my office. She looked excruciatingly lovely as she walked toward me, her skin diaphanous, her eyes a clear blue. Thick straight hair framed her oval face and she moved with slender grace. I held her in a tight embrace, murmuring, "Ma petite fille, ma chérie." She sat, ate a few spoonfuls of soup. I still see her thin fingers wrapped around the thick brown coffee cup.

How do you make conversation with your drowning daughter on her twentieth birthday? She assured me that she was safe, that she stayed with friends. Maybe, I thought. She assured me that she was clean, that she did not need treatment. I did not believe her. Her expression was empty and as slick as a con's. She promised to call, told me not to worry, that she'd be all right, and stood up. "She is wrong, dead wrong," I thought with horror as I watched her cross the room, open the door, and leave.

Her psychiatrist had just left on vacation, so I called the person who covered her practice. This doctor didn't know Luce personally, so could not intervene, but we talked of what might be done to protect her, as I was certain she had relapsed. The doctor called the head of the psychiatric hospital where Luce had been two weeks before, and asked if he would request from the Court a temporary hold for involuntary treatment. He refused, saying that when he'd last examined Luce he did not think she was suicidal and, not having examined her since, he had no evidence to present to a judge that she now was. Which was true of course. We were on our own, helpless and powerless.

Later we learned that Luce went to Anna's that day and asked to live with her and Rick. Anna, in tears, refused. "I saw too many junkies when I lived in New York. I know they'll do anything, they'll steal, they'll lie. You are a junkie Luce, and as long as you're not clean, you can't live with us. After you finish treatment maybe, but I can't live with someone I can't trust."

In the early morning following her birthday, Luce walked back to Sobriety First. "I know I can't live this way," she said. "This time

I'm asking for treatment on my own. I need to get back to my program."

James and I met her there to go through admission proceedings again. "I know too much," she said, "I can't use denial anymore even when I'm on heroin. So even that doesn't work for me anymore."

That's when she gave me the rock, the one with the fine lines pressed together by the weight of eons, telling me that's what addiction was. "It's like each of these lines is the bar of a prison and they press on me with an awful strength and I can't get out and I can't be free. I am crushed."

She went to every lecture, participated in every group. She was awesomely honest, said the other patients, and helped them a lot. But day by day she lost weight, strength, energy. It seemed that the light of life in her dimmed little by little, inexorably.

The staff rallied around Luce. They wanted her to make it. The nurses put her in a bed across from their station, in a room by herself, and dropped in often with encouraging words. Yet they saw her lose ground, get more and more distant. Her psychiatrist, back from vacation, prescribed an increase in antidepressant medication and again we discussed if she should be in a different facility. But once more, at a staff meeting, all of us together reasoned that one would only know the true depth of her depression and be able to treat it appropriately after she'd been drug free for at least several days, past the withdrawal. The whole situation was very confusing. At that point, I couldn't think straight. I was only a fearful mom and deferred to the other professionals.

James visited Luce during the day. He was almost happy when he called me after their conversations. "She sounds really committed and she's honest. I think she can make it." He had faith in her courage and the strength of the Twelve-Step program.

In the evenings, I stopped by after work. Luce would be in bed, stretched incredibly thin under the covers, immobile. She was always cold, often asleep. I lay beside her, taking her in my arms and stretching myself all along her body to warm her. She'd wake but not move.

She spoke in whispers. "I am so scared, Mom. I don't know if I can make it. I feel so bad."

"Bad how? Do you mean guilty?"

"No. I feel small. So small I can't do anything."

I told her it was a terrible time to go through, but it would pass, she'd get better. I don't know if I believed it, but I wouldn't let her see my doubts.

Each night, she seemed diminished.

The nurses told me that as the week went on she spent more and more time in bed, not moving, except to go to group therapy. They said that she perked up when her father or I came to visit. "By the time you leave, she glows. But then it goes away. It lasts about twenty minutes." So we each spent as much time as we could with her, separately to make it last longer.

Anna and David did not come. They hated hospitals, didn't know what to say to Luce, and waited for her return home to pick up where they left off.

On November 13, the air was clear and the autumn foliage glowed gold in the sun. James and I persuaded Luce to come for a walk with us in the quiet Sunday streets. She walked as if she were ninety years old, slow and unsteady, and we each held her hand as she shuffled around the block. Only one block, and it took forever. She seemed not to notice the sun, the colors, or the sharp yeasty smell of fallen leaves. She looked almost blind, and so frail.

"I don't know if I can do this any longer," she said.

"Walk?"

"No, live. I don't have the strength."

Back in her narrow room, her dad and I sat very close on each side of her on the white metal bed. We held her as she cried and trembled. "It's too hard. I can't go on." We all huddled together as if James and I could transfuse strength and hope into her, and protect her by the power of our love.

"Sweetheart," I said, "if I knew it would condemn you to this kind of pain forever, I wouldn't ask you to go on. But look at me.

You know that I wanted to die, very badly, when I was your age. And I've had a good life. You know I'm happy, don't you?"

"Yes, I know."

I tried to lift her spirit by adding in a lighthearted tone, "Remember, a few years back, you said you wanted to have my life. To be a doctor and have children. Well, you can. This will end, you'll see."

James also gave words of comfort. "We'll stand by you. I want what's best for you and I trust you."

Luce looked up at each of us in turn with a sad, faint smile. But it was a smile. We both felt better when we got home. We had succeeded in comforting ourselves.

When I went to visit Luce from my office after work on Monday, she was nowhere to be found. Nobody remembered seeing her at dinner. She had probably walked out just after an afternoon group therapy session.

We know nothing of the next day. Nobody we know saw her, she called no one we've met since. She had no money, no home. The previous night, after discovering that she'd left Sobriety First, James and I had driven through all the neighborhoods where we thought she might be, looking on streets and into alleys. We called her friends, called the detective. Anna and David also looked for her late into the night.

When Luce was at the hospital by the jail, she had told us during a family meeting what she'd learned from her previous suicide attempts. After I pointed out that she must want to live because she'd let us know when she was in danger, she acknowledged that she had sent signals which allowed us to intervene and save her. But she added: "Next time I decide to kill myself, I won't mess it up. I'll do it right." Of course there was no way to know if this would be the time, but the words rang unbearably in my head.

I cancelled my work appointments on Tuesday and went to the drug house where Luce had told me her friend took her the time he introduced her to heroin. It was a big, square, respectable-looking house, which has since been torn down and was probably used by squatters then. I waited on the deep unlit porch a long time after ringing the doorbell.

The girl who opened was very pale and skinny, with thin black clothes and piercings that caught the light. I asked for the boy Luce knew. "Nobody here by that name," she said. I smelled incense and saw candlelight beyond a door to the right. I thought I saw people there, lying on futons on the floor.

"Do you have a girl here? Luce. I'd like to come in and look for her."

"You can't."

An Indian bedspread in a doorway fluttered and a young man, also very thin, came from another room. The girl turned to him.

"You have to go," he said firmly, very black eyes looking hard at me, and he closed the door in my face.

I returned home in a daze and told James. We couldn't just sit and wait. We went to her empty apartment, to her former work, the coffee shops she liked, all the places we could think of. The two of us, plus David and Anna, called all the people we knew Luce to be connected to, plus others we guessed she might have crossed paths with, whom she'd known in childhood, met in the program or at school.

In the end, as night fell, James and I sat at home with David, talking to each other and by phone to close friends, trying not to go crazy with fear. Until finally, having exhausted all avenues, we went to bed. My mind swam between near-sleep and jarring thoughts of more places to go or people to reach, my heart racing, as if I hadn't already done all that.

When the doorbell rang, a half-hour past midnight, we both gasped and bolted at the same time, with the same thought: Luce! She made her way home. I pulled on a robe while James ran to the door.

I didn't see the policeman who stood there, who, when James opened the door, told him they'd found Luce. That she was dead. He would write in his report, "The father was momentarily overcome by emotion." From the bedroom, I heard James scream in agony, and all hope bled from me.

I rushed to the hallway where James and I clasped hands hard enough to hurt, while the policeman told us what he knew. They had been called at ten-thirty p.m. by the manager of Luce's studio. The tenant in the adjacent apartment had heard noises and, knowing that the place was supposed to be vacant, called management to report. The manager came in and found the body.

We moved without plan, drifting into the kitchen. Out of habit, James went to the coffee machine and brewed a pot. We sat around the kitchen table, James and the cop with coffee cups in front of them. Tears fell on my hands, yet I was not aware of crying. My eyes fastened on the officer's face as if he alone could make sense of this insanity, the unbridgeable chasm between worrying about my daughter dying and knowing that death had just eaten her.

The officer was a nice young man, mid-thirties, soft-spoken. He sat with both hands around the coffee cup, his hat on the table next to it. He was obviously moved, saddened by the news he brought, but also stiff, reticent.

"Where is she?" As if it made a difference.

"How did she die?" I don't know which of us asked the questions. James and I were of one mind.

"The body is at the morgue. We're pretty sure it was an overdose. There was a note."

"What does it say?

"It's addressed to you both."

"Do you have it?"

He straightened his shoulders but kept his short-cropped head slightly bowed, eyes on the table, not our faces. He spoke slowly. "We have to wait for the coroner's report."

"Coroner's report?"

"It's almost certainly suicide, but we need an autopsy to rule out foul play."

Images of a dissected body flashed in my mind. "Can I see her? Before the autopsy?"

"You have to get permission from the coroner. Autopsy is scheduled for tomorrow morning." He told me the coroner's name, a pathologist at the hospital, and his number. I got up to bring pen and paper, and asked him to write it, knowing I could never remember. Then he continued. "After we get his report, if it's suicide, we'll give you the note. Your daughter's clothes are in the apartment. The manager will let you in if you want." He wrote that phone number too.

I nodded. I wanted to see as much as possible, as if details could give me clues, make sense of the horrifying act. Or of its devastating consequence, the infinite absence of our daughter. My mind could not begin to touch that, let alone apprehend or comprehend it. Luce was gone. Luce as a person did not exist. The world could not be right, my universe could not be conceived of, without her existence. It could not be. When I recall those moments, it's as if I were looking through a tiny, crystal-clear window through which my eyes and factual mind recorded every detail, but the rest of me was a heavy mass of unspeakable, unknowable emotions.

The policeman left. James and I held each other close and tight, standing in silence for the longest time. We did not bother to wipe our tears or runny noses. There was a great rushing sound inside me.

When we parted, James went to sit in the living room and I went to bed. Not to sleep, but because I could no longer stand. All strength gone, I floated, not feeling my own body. No thoughts came: I had lost my mind. Yet I was fully awake, fully aware that Luce was gone, and tears kept flowing. My eyes hurt, my face hurt, there was nothing to be done.

Hours passed and I could not summon an image of her, not a glimpse of her dear face. I had completely lost her, even the memories. I felt despair, total emptiness. Then a sensation began in my belly where the womb had pulsed with her life twenty years before. I felt the swelling, the mounding, the heft and weight of it. I felt the movements of her body inside its pouch of silken redness, her limbs stretching, the press of her head against the opening.

My body remembered, slowly, in real time it seemed. The sensations were so luxuriant and welcome that different tears, warm and healing, mixed with the bitter ones. I floated in the remembering.

I envisioned the cervix flattening, opening like a mouth in wonder. The powerful contractions of the uterus evoked kneading fingers. It was as if a hand pressed on the infant's bottom to move her forward, nudging her firmly toward her destiny. And after the head pushed its way through as stubbornly as a little goat's, after the body slivered out in a tangle of slippery limbs, I felt her mouth drawing milk from my breast, her wriggly naked small weight on my chest.

When light seeped in through the slats of the window shade, tracing pale lines on the yellow wall, I got up to join James. His face was ruined by tears, swollen under the reddened eyes, slashed by deep cracks, his useless arms and hands hung from defeated shoulders. The weight of his grief on top of mine made me stagger and I wanted to remove myself from his sight so that my own pain would not crush him. But we sat together to plan for the day.

The children would have to be told, also his parents and our friends, sisters, and brothers. But first I wanted to be sure that we could see Luce a last time. I called the hospital and the medical examiner authorized us to go to the morgue. He said we had to come early as the autopsy was scheduled for eight a.m. He also gave us advice on how to arrange for the cremation we decided on.

We woke David who came in a daze to join us as we called Anna. I have no recollection of how David looked or of what Anna said on the phone. I wasn't able to absorb their feelings, to imagine what it was for them to lose their sister. I suspect that David stayed silent, as he often did.

When telling Anna and David of the opportunity to see Luce's body, we made it clear that we thought there was no right or wrong way to respond. That they should decide for themselves, but they must do it very fast. Neither has regretted that decision since. David would come with us, Anna would not. Rick was at her side and I trusted the strength of his devotion. When Anna said she'd be all right, I believed her.

Luce lay on a gurney at the center of a small gray room under a bright ceiling light. The room was completely empty. She was covered by a sheet up to the top of her breasts, arms lying at her sides over the sheet. Her dark hair was brushed back from her face, her high forehead glistening. I'd had horrific visions of violence done to her body during the long day when she was missing; she could have thrown herself from a building, she could have been beaten, murdered. Comforted to see her intact, I approached to touch her. I placed a hand over hers, kissed her face.

But of course it was not her. The skin was waxy and cold, the fingers stiff. The color of her face was off, bluish with a darker hue by the ears, along the edge of the slackened cheeks. The profile remained familiar, the thin straight nose, full mouth, and narrow chin. I caressed the thick hair; it felt unchanged, as did the black arched eyebrows. It moved me again to see the right eyebrow going up like a small wing at the top of the arc. My hand went lightly over a shoulder, an arm; they felt like smooth marble, the whole body like a funereal statue on a tomb.

David, James, and I stood immobile for a time out of time, looking at Luce's face, each with a hand on her, reaching toward the unattainable. Someone knocked and came in to signal the end of the visit, and we left in deep silence.

AFTER

What do you do when the stakes are so high and you've already lost? Anything you could say now dissipates like smoke. It's too late, it's done. Your loudest scream will not be heard, the scream that would've brought her back from the edge of the abyss. The game was played and lost long ago. Yet you don't want to be silent. The roar is in your throat, the scream of warning will have to be thrown even if it tears your voice, even as it rips your throat.

As if constantly on the lookout for traces of her, I recognized Luce in this or that young woman and I thought for a crazed instant that my voice or my hand could reach her. Here is what I wrote in May 1997:

SMITHEREENS

What happened?

Your body at the morgue seemed
solid, marmoreal,
compact and distant.
Yet I saw your wide front teeth
today,
in the grin of a young woman

laughing with her friend.
I wanted to shake her by the shoulders,
hard!
"Where did you get those?
What did you do to her?"
then, softly:
"Do you know where she is,
where I can find her?"

Your death seemed simple,
nothing to wonder about,
finite.
I imagined Life as a great lake,
illuminated by the spirit
to produce the shimmer of you,
perfect, beautiful,
gone.
But I saw,
I swear I saw,
your gleaming straight hair
on a girl drinking coffee
on 13th by the bookstore.
My hand left my side,
avid,
to stroke her head,
the imagined caress
flooding me
with intolerable longing.

I did not have to imagine
the Earth claiming your body,
Fire did.
Holding its ashes was odd:
not the fine weightless matter
I had imagined,
but a thick soapy density,

disturbing—I don't know why,
and there were the bits of bone
which still spoke of you,
real, you,
not an image.
It is not so easy to obliterate a life,
my little vandal.

Where were you when your father and I,
in Denver,
both stopped,
heart in our throat,
and checked each other,
his eyes wide, confirming what I saw?
She was nervous,
elegant and tense,
chin tilted up.
Her eyes were dark and hair curly
but we knew, we knew
that it was you at thirty-five.
The long thighs, round rump,
right hip cocked forward,
in slim black leather pants
and boots you would have died for,
the shoulders and neck straight in a fine
black leather jacket,
Italian for sure,
expressed all your ambition,
your drive.
This was you, who would have
traveled the world
with Doctors Without Borders
and shopped in Milan on the way back.

So, tell me,
what happened?

Did you at the moment of your death
blow to smithereens,
embedding the universe
with little shards of you
which I have to discover
in a sickening game of Hide and Seek?

For several years I could not appreciate the relief from being freed of wondering what I should do for my daughter, or what would happen to her next. No decision needed to be taken on her behalf any longer. But what is the good of surviving the confusion of a train crash, only to find oneself pinned under the wreck? Such is the grief I could not get out from under. I could pretend at times to be happy for Luce that she no longer hurt. But I hurt. All the time.

Every decision I'd made during her illness could be used to flagellate myself. Particularly the choice of the local treatment center in the last month of her life, over the very expensive, but highly superior, hospital where I'd been trained. I replayed arguments that appeared cogent at the time: protecting Anna and David was essential, and sending Luce alone halfway across the country would have torn her and us. Nevertheless, I was furious.

Would taking Luce to Kansas have saved her life? Could it have? I wanted to scream and tear at myself with these words: "You didn't try hard enough. You didn't take care of her, do everything you could. Shame on you to say you loved this child more than life itself. You protected yourselves, you chose your comfort, life after her, even before she died."

I wailed inside. "Damn me for that. And damn you, Luce, for being so intransigent, for refusing to compromise, to accept your lot, to live with what you had."

Yet what if she'd lived and there had only been more confusion and heartache for all from then on? I knew well the families of several of her friends and contemporaries who'd had to deal during all these years with the seesaw of repeated attempts at recovery, various treatment programs, followed by shattering relapses and near suicides. What did any of us know of what could've been? Yet I couldn't help indulge in the futile exercise of wondering.

David also felt guilty, mostly for his decision not to visit Luce at Sobriety First. He was unable to tell anyone for almost a year after her death, until it ate him up and he became despondent. Finally he told us, "You know, all my life it seems like she was in the hospital. She'd be very sick, and then she'd get better, and then she got out. I figured I'd see her when she got out." His dad and I told him that we thought this point of view made total sense with what he knew then. He seemed reassured by the time he left for engineering school in Colorado.

Even if no calendar existed, the change of light would tell me when the season of pain and regret begins. I am a hostage of history and love. October and November bring memories of Luce's suffering and of our dismay. The memories get more focused, the grief sharper, as the days pass, and the week between her birthday on November 7 and the day when she died on November 15 gives a foreshortened view of her life. She takes center stage.

I schedule nothing for November 15. The whole day is open to whatever comes. And that is different every year. On the third anniversary, in 1997, I woke with an intense regret that I had not been with Luce when she died, that she had to die alone.

It was not the first time I thought that. It broke my heart to imagine her alone, naked in a barren place. I wished I could have given her the comfort of a hand holding hers, of a word of love. I knew full well, of course, that this couldn't have happened. Had I been there, I would have taken her in my arms, murmured in her ear, "Hang on, you've been there before, you'll get better." I would've fought with her to keep her alive, as would have any other person who loved her. Luce's decision to kill herself included dying alone.

I woke up, three years later, overwhelmed by the sadness that it had to be so. Then, knowing that in the realm of emotions time is not linear, I decided that I would hold Luce's hand through her last day and through the time of her death. I reminded myself of every detail of her last hours that I'd learned over the years.

She wrote her suicide note to us on lined paper with three holes on the side and "Notes" printed at the top, like some of the sheets I found in her Sobriety First patient folder. She might have written it before leaving and carried it in her pocket. It was dated 11/14, her last day at Sobriety First, written in green ink, folded in four.

> I know I am an addict. I know this disease is terminal. I've been trying to do it for friends and family. Well—Family; Because I love you and I know you love me. The problem is—I just don't care about myself enough. I'm sorry. All I can say is some day, please forgive me. My life has just been so much pain . . .
>
> I'm sorry. L

How long did it take her to come up with a plan? Had it been in place since she left the psychiatric hospital? She'd told Anna about buying a gun soon after leaving her father and me in front of the jail.

Because Luce did not break in to enter her former apartment, I presumed she had hidden a key somewhere close by and made sure the place hadn't been rented to somebody else. How did she buy the heroin? She'd had no money in her wallet when an inventory was made at the time of her last admission at Sobriety First. It was probable that she'd hidden the gun with the apartment key and sold it or exchanged it for heroin.

When I went to her apartment the day after she died, I was moved to see her clothes neatly folded in a pile in the empty room, as the policeman told us they found them. At home, I had asked Luce over and over to pick up her clothes. Seeing them folded convinced me that it was an act of love, that as she undressed she chose to leave the least amount of mess for us to see. It echoed the tone of her note, which had been propped up on the bathroom sink "facing the door to be read by anyone entering," said the police report, of which we'd requested a copy.

Luce's body was found in the bathtub in a few inches of water.

Police found a ring of brown residue in a spoon, new syringes on a shelf in the kitchen. I imagined that she laid herself in the bathtub because there was no bed and that she drew hot water because there was no heat. The warmth would also make it easier to find a vein. A syringe was found on the sill of the tub, a blue sash cord beside it and brownish residue in the syringe barrel.

The conclusion of the medical examiner was: "The cause of death is attributed to acute opiate intoxication. The manner of death is determined to be suicide."

Luce did not die immediately. The pathologist found acute bronchopneumonia due to the aspiration into the lungs of vomit, a little of which was still in her mouth. The neighbor told the police that he'd heard loud snoring or moaning as much as an hour before he called the manager.

That detail was particularly grievous because all of us had taken comfort in the image of Luce dying immediately, in a burst of euphoria, finding the peace she sought. She was probably not conscious during her last hour, but who knows about the space between life and death?

In the dark years after her death I had often perceived myself as immersed in the black waters of the river Styx, the boundary between the dead and the living as imagined by ancient Greeks. They thought that the souls of the dead were ferried across it to their new residence.

I even had the desultory thought of trying heroin myself, to know what that thing was, which had been worth dying for. To meet her sweet assassin. To share the experience with my own sweet daughter, who now drew me toward death.

I had stopped work five months after she died because I didn't feel able to safely take care of the severely self-destructive patients I treated. Not only was I assaulted by my own horrid memories when I listened to them, but I noticed a dangerous shift in me. Hearing of one woman's constant battle with suicidal impulses, I thought, Hasn't she suffered enough? Why doesn't she give up? I became certain that, over time, my patient would sense how my resolve to fight for her life had weakened. And I was terrified of the consequences.

Another patient told me, on the tenth anniversary of her own suicide attempt, "I have been able to resist all those years because you've been on my side. But since your daughter died, you're not as strong and I think I'll kill myself." Her words stabbed me, but she was right and I convinced her to work with another doctor. My patients needed someone stronger, not submerged in the cold swirls of grief.

In 1997, on the third anniversary of Luce's death, I understood that I had not allowed her to complete her journey across the river Styx. Like a hand gripping an arm, my questions held her close. "Answer me. Why did you have to do this? Why couldn't you have waited? Trusted? We could've found a way to make you feel better. You were just a kid, you didn't know enough to make the deadly choice. I could have taught you how one lives with the enemy within."

But I couldn't forget the evenings when I held her in my arms, the last week of her life, on her bed at the treatment center. It didn't seem that she was seeking union with a death that resided outside of her, as I had thought she did during her adolescence. I hadn't grasped it then but, looking back, it felt as if death were inside her, part of the very fabric of her being, coursing through her body as if she had leukemia.

I also recalled something reported by the counselor who led the last group therapy session she'd attended, just before walking out of the place. In group, Luce told the other members that her parents had given her permission to live or to die. Had we, had I? I don't know. I replayed the sentences James and I spoke after the Sunday walk, intended to encourage. Had she not smiled upon hearing them? Should I feel guilty if she received another message from my words? Or comforted that she did not see us as enemies at the time of her death?

On the morning of November 15, 1997, in my room, I decided that I would no longer ask the silent questions, I wouldn't exhort or plead. To stay by her, symbolically, to the end, I had to give her the only comfort she asked for in her note: my loving forgiveness. I had to love her, including that awful decision that I hated. I had to respect that it was hers to make, even as it wrecked my life.

I summoned all the power of love to stay focused on her as I imagined her last moments. As if I crouched close to the tub where she lay and held my breath while she pulled the dissolved drug into the syringe, found a vein swollen by the warm water, and pushed the poison in. As if I held her hand after it dropped the syringe, until the fingers went limp and I knew she had crossed onto her death. Then I opened my own fingers and felt her slip away in the dark.

I found myself alone, cold and shivering, and remained quiet for a moment of profound stillness. Then I stood up and went for a walk in the woods. It was as if I had left the cold waters and climbed back to the bank to stand on the land of the living. The thought "Death is in the order of things" presented itself repeatedly to my mind during this walk. It would accompany me in the years to come and give me solace.

Above my desk, I pinned a magazine photo of an Algerian woman who'd just lost all of her family to a terrorist assault on her village during the recent civil war. Her wide-open wailing mouth and tightly shut eyes mirrored my anguish in the days after Luce's death. Glancing at the picture reminded me that I am the unexceptional member of a vast sisterhood of bereaved mothers.

And I remember the quote from Aeschylus carved on Robert Kennedy's tombstone: "Even in our sleep, pain which cannot forget falls drop by drop upon the heart, until, in our own despair, against our will, comes wisdom by the awful grace of God."

Since then, grief is as deep as ever when I feel it. But it is not as wide. It no longer covers the whole world. For a long time I could remember nothing of Luce's life except the last months. Grief on top of grief, I'd lost all of her but the suffering. Not all the memories of previous joys have returned and I don't know that they ever will. Like a scintillating shimmer of sunlight on the surface of the clear lake of timelessness, Luce's existence appeared, captured my heart, changed in too swift a moment, and was gone.

For months after her death, I was best soothed by listening to Johann Sebastian Bach's *Goldberg Variations*, bathed in the music, without any notion of what in this appeased my pain. Only years later did I understand, when I heard the music anew in all its depth.

In the dark of a small concert hall, tears swelled in my burning eyes before the dam broke, and I thought I might choke and have to leave the room. But the friend beside me, who'd known my children as well as I knew hers, took my hand and we sailed into the music together, tears and all. Peace grew in me throughout the tumultuous journey and, for a long time after the pianist had left the stage, I lingered in my seat, flooded with gratitude.

Only the next morning, alone and taking in the first light of day, did I grasp the meaning of this experience. Bach gives every emotion its due in the successive parts of the piece. He seems to abandon himself to a feeling, not shrinking from its intensity, but the form remains highly structured, suggesting there may be order in what cannot be controlled. He contains the emotion just as he expresses it. At one moment he yields to sadness, slow and soft, the next he flies into a torrid dance. Utter pain is there, and also joy.

SINCE

In the years of brutal grief, David, Anna, James, and I huddled very close, tender to each other. Then, over time, the children moved away and James and I pursued healing apart from each other.

We have full, separate, and connected lives. Anna and her husband Rick have built a strong family and their daughters know Luce by name. David is also married and joy courses through him as it did before Luce became ill. When James and I, now divorced, meet at family events, I am grateful that we can share joys and tragedies as a loving unit.

Retired, I spend more time in France and have renewed meaningful ties there. But I couldn't conceive of leaving the United States, entirely mine after so many years, a home I share with my children and trustworthy friends.

I am buoyed by the power of life. In the end, beauty, love, discoveries have healed my wounds. Seducing me like a lover through precious minute touches, life had its way with me.

I am happy.

Yet, at times, I wonder if this is dumb or wise. Here I am, an old woman, living alone and far, far away from where I was born. And I am happy? I don't get it. When I wake up and feel a smile on my lips, I shake my head, puzzled.

Some days, still, a racing heart wakes me as if I were running barely ahead of the monsters that have carved their marks on my flesh. Have I learned nothing from the days of pain and fear? Could happiness be a trick, a soporific that softens focus and judgment? As if fate handed me a laced drink and I smiled sweetly while sipping it. Eros and Thanatos, the pulls of life and death, working in tandem, toying with me. One lures me while the other licks its chops in anticipation.

I can throw myself into experience, do what comes next and pay the price, if it comes to that. I just can't forget that the price may be stiff. Eros bows to Thanatos, death is woven into life. Which does not detract from the beauty of the whole.

Most days, I respond to the new light with pleasure. I rise to meet the day even if I'm not certain I should trust it. I could conceive of fate and destiny as did the ancient Greeks, in the shape of the gods of Olympus who captured my imagination when I was a schoolgirl. Beautiful and dramatic, driven by grand appetites and passions, they often acted without good reasons.

I remind myself that their forefather, before Chronos, was Chaos. There are so many things I don't get, that I can't understand. Still, fascinated by the unknowable that surrounds the little I can see, I am compelled to look at the edges where light plays with darkness. And I prefer coming close to the mysteries, even if I get singed brushing against them.

After my suicide attempt, I discovered at the Louvre the self-portrait Albrecht Dürer painted at twenty-two, and I kept a postcard of this painting on my wall for the rest of my twenties. In it, Dürer is a mature young man who turns his head toward the mirror he used—now the viewer. Light catches on his strong nose, high cheekbones, and naked neck. Red hair falls to his shoulders and a black cloak open to the waist reveals a white muslin shirt gathered in fine pleats over his powerful torso. He is handsome, radiant.

But what kept me hooked, unable to walk away, was his gaze. In it, I read no threat, no challenge, no seduction. His full mouth neither smiled nor turned down in bitterness. The intense, straight-on curiosity in his green eyes seemed to pull the man forward, to a life of passionate examination of what is, which I meant to emulate.

Many years later, a long while after Luce's death, I visited the Sistine Chapel. The colors on Michelangelo's ceiling shone bright after a recent restoration.

I surprised myself by bursting into tears as soon as I looked up. My tears were not triggered by the figure of the Creator, as they might have been when I was young and prone to mysticism.

Instead, I was moved by the gesture of Adam receiving his life, and fate, with consummate grace and good will, extending a hand to be touched by God's finger. His is an almost nonchalant acceptance, as if he said, "Alright, I don't know what I'm signing up for, but I'll go for it."

I read in his benignly skeptical yet uncritical expression a heartbreaking trust toward the unknown, unknowable source from which the life given to him emanates. To me, by so doing, he is the personification of human dignity in the face of our inherent smallness.

And so do I wish to live every day.

www.ingramcontent.com/pod-product-compliance
Lightning Source LLC
Chambersburg PA
CBHW021829020426
42334CB00014B/555